FOCUS ON THE FAMILY

P9-BYN-393

TRIBE

A Warrior's Heart

Michael Ross

TYNDALE

Tyndale House Publishers, Inc.
Wheaton, Illinois

ISBN: 1-58997-118-3

A Focus on the Family book published by
Tyndale House Publishers, Wheaton, Illinois 60189

Focus on the Family books are available at special quantity discounts when purchased in bulk by corporations, organizations, churches, or groups. For more information, contact: Focus on the Family, 8605 Explorer Drive, Colorado Springs, CO 80920; or phone (800) 932-9123.

Editor: Mick Silva
Cover & interior design: Tom Hook
Cover photo: Stockbyte
Rock Climbing photo and Summit photo: Gaylon Wampler

Printed in the United States of America
1 2 3 4 5 6 7 8 9 /09 08 07 06 05 04

To Christopher, my son:
I love you, I'm proud of you, and I'll never stop thanking God for you.
I pray that you'll always stay close to Him during your journey.

"There is a way into my country from all the worlds. . . . I will not tell you how long or short the way will be; only that it lies across the river. But do not fear that, for I am the great Bridge Builder."
—Aslan, *Voyage of the Dawn Treader*
C.S. Lewis

CONTENTS

CONTENTS CONTINUED

ACKNOWLEDGMENTS

Michael Ross would like to thank the following people and publishers for their involvement with this book:

Greg Hartman for writing about Neil Armstrong and Buzz Aldrin in the Day 2 entry.

Mary Spaulding for lending research and insights about the life of John Wesley in the Day 9 entry.

Todd Huston for sharing his story in the Day 10 entry.

Zondervan for giving permission to reprint the story about Samson in the Day 11 entry. A portion of this chapter was adapted from *Men of the Bible* by Ann Spangler and Robert Wolgemuth, © 2002, Zondervan.

Barbour Publishing for giving permission to reprint the story about Samuel Morris in the Day 13 entry. A portion of this chapter was adapted from *Samuel Morris: The Apostle of Simple Faith,* by W. Terry Whalin, © 1996, Barbour Publishing.

Manfred Koehler for contributing to the story about Jesus Christ in the Day 18 entry.

Bill Myers for contributing to the stories about Jesus Christ in the Day 17, 19 and 20 entries.

Jim Ware for contributing to the story about C.S. Lewis in the Day 26 entry. A portion of this chapter was adapted from his book *God of the Fairy Tale,* © 2003, Shaw Books.

Tiffany Ross for putting into practice her seminary education and lending theological insights to this entire book!

Introduction: The Journey

A young Hobbit studies the ring in his hand, wondering how it came to him, questioning his ability to handle the journey. *Why me? I'm just a Hobbit—simple, quiet . . . unimportant. How can I be trusted with such a difficult task?*

Frodo Baggins isn't a warrior like Aragorn. He isn't powerful like Gandalf. He isn't even brave like Gimli, the feisty Dwarf. Yet Frodo has been chosen for a dangerous quest, an adventure that will transform his life and ultimately rescue Middle Earth.

He shivers at everything Gandalf has just told him about this terrible ring. The One Ring. The Ring of Power. It was thought to be lost, but is now desperately sought by its maker, the dreaded Dark Lord. This magical piece of jewelry threatened to overpower everyone and everything, to change Middle Earth forever.

And this ring has somehow found its way into Frodo's hands.

Yet even though he has to leave the Shire—all that is safe and familiar—Frodo actually looks forward to traveling. He *wants* to have adventures like his uncle Bilbo. He often imagines himself taking long, aimless journeys

through endless woods, splashing across fabled rivers, and camping under the stars.

But this! This is greater than anything he ever dreamed of. *I was not made for such an important quest. Why me?*

Frodo is up to his ears in adventure because of his loyalty to his friends and family—*his tribe*—not to mention four simple words he spoke earlier: "What must I do?"

What must I do, Gandalf? I may be small and weak and unimportant—but how can I help? What is expected of me?

What's that, Gandalf? You're asking me to save Middle Earth? You're asking this tiny Hobbit to suddenly transform into a giant . . . to do the impossible?

• • •

Impossible! I tell myself as I cling to a steep rock face. *I'm not Spider-Man! How'd I ever get talked into this?*

I'm on a 10-day backpacking trip in California's Ansel Adams Wilderness with a bunch of *Breakaway* guys—teen boys who read the magazine I edit each month. We're undergoing a "tribal quest."

Today's challenge: Scale a slick canyon wall.

I slide my right hand across a boulder and feel a tiny crevice. I grip it with my fingertips and push with my legs.

As I inch my way up the wall (and begin to trust the safety harness around my waist) I quickly discover that this climb isn't all that crazy, after all. The only really scary part is wearing a blindfold. That's right, a bandanna is covering my eyes. I can't see a thing!

"Excellent, Mike! You're doing great," a voice yells up from below. It's my friend Tom Hook the guy who designed this book. He's my climbing partner and, quite literally, my eyes during this exercise.

"Listen to my voice," Tom says. "I'll get you to the top. Trust me."

I reach above my head and dig my fingers into another crevice.

"That's it," Tom shouts. "Now push with your legs again. Another three feet and you're there."

I'm way out of my comfort zone. In fact, I've been living on the edge all week—pushing my body and tuning in to God.

Suddenly, chaos. I can't hear Tom's voice and some of the other guys are attempting to guide me in different directions.

"Go to the left," someone yells.

"No—move to your right."

"Push harder with your legs."

Tom comes to the rescue: "Quiet!" After a few seconds of silence, I hear his voice again. "Listen to me. Reach for a handhold above your head, push with your legs and you'll be at the top."

His instructions are perfect. Before I realize it, I've reached my destination. Victory! I hear applause from other members of my tribe. I pull off the bandanna, feeling confident, and look down.

Should have stuck with the blindfold!

• • •

Often in life we face difficult quests, even dangerous ones with life-altering outcomes: standing up for what's right instead of what's popular, leading a friend to Christ, saying "no" to stuff that can harm us (drugs, premarital sex, negative peer pressure).

But sometimes, the task at hand is a bit less risky (and a lot more fun) conquering our fears on a rock face.

Regardless of what's asked of us at any given moment, understand that *life itself is a journey.* Your very existence on Planet Earth is an amazing adventure filled with countless surprises, thrills, challenges, choices, and so much promise. But as you begin to launch out on your own life quests, ask yourself one very important question: Are you anchored to the solid rock of God and His Word?

With each choice you make, are you "belayed" (or supported) by the Holy Spirit who is pointing out solid holds and ready to catch you if you fall? Or are you dangerously hanging from loose, rotten rock that is slowly crumbling away.

Answering these questions depends upon the tribe you identify with—especially your *tribal creed,* the beliefs and values your tribe holds dear.

The features of our tribal identity are unique:

GOD'S TRIBAL MEMBERSHIP CREED

1. *I have undergone the rite of passage.* Guys are inducted into the group only after undergoing a rite—which often involves a physical challenge that proves the initiate's changed spirit and willingness to subvert his identity to the group. *Members of God's tribe (1) submit their lives to Jesus Christ, (2) commit to His authority and power, and (3) join His body of believers.*

2. *I accept the sacred text.* Personal identity is bound to a Statement of Belief. *Members of God's tribe follow the absolute truth of the Holy Bible.*

3. *I enter into a lifelong membership.* Tribal members are "branded" by their forfeit of individual identity and become absolutely loyal to the group. *Members of God's tribe make a 180-degree change of heart that is absolutely, 100% permanent.*

4. *I attend council meetings consistently.* Regular meetings ensure the bond within the group and further the dominion of the tribe's goals. *Members of God's tribe make church a priority.*

5. *I fulfill my individual responsibilities.* Unique tasks are assigned to every member, both to reinforce respect and commitment to the tribe's goals and creed, and to strengthen the tribe. *Members of God's tribe desire what makes them "come alive in Christ" and strive to fit their lives into the Creator's perfect plan.*

Okay. So what exactly is this you're getting into? Is this a devotional? Is it a journal? Is it a journey? Actually, yes to all of the above!

In each daily entry you'll find:

• **TRIBAL QUEST**—a faith challenge for the day.

• **TRIBAL TRUTH**—Scripture that defines a Christian's tribal quest.

• **TRIBAL FACE**—a true account of a faith hero who sought after God's heart and earned himself a new identity in God's worldwide tribe. These heroes include astronauts and coal miners, missionaries, martyrs, outcasts, and emperors.

• **TRIBAL TRAINING**—advice, action-points, and thought-provoking questions and strategies for applying God's truth to your life.

• **TRIBAL MARKS**—plenty of space to journal and write out your own

prayers, thoughts, hopes . . . and all the new stuff you've learned.

So, don't hold back! Fulfill what burns in every young man's heart. Dare to trust your Creator and become the warrior He made you to be. Use this life-changing resource as a way to get connected to God's eternal tribe.

Study with a friend or group of guys from church—maybe even your dad (you know, as your own tribal rite-of-passage thing). Just remember: When you reach out to your Creator and ask with a sincere heart, "What must I do, Lord? What is expected of me?"—be ready to plunge in headfirst! Your ultimate journey awaits. Join the adventure of following Christ. And with each quest He gives you, don't be surprised if you find yourself facing—and overcoming—challenges far greater than anything you ever imagined.

Joining God's Inner Circle

WEEKLY MEMORY VERSE

Then Jesus said to his disciples, "If anyone would come after me, he must deny himself and take up his cross and follow me. For whoever wants to save his life will lose it, but whoever loses his life for me will find it."

—Matthew 16:24–25

FOLLOW ME

Day 1: "Come, Follow Me!"

» TRIBAL QUEST

Move beyond religion and "head knowledge" and experience a deeper bond with Jesus Christ, striving to grow daily in His love, power, and truth. *Explore the Word: Matthew 4:18–22; 16:13–17:9.*

» TRIBAL TRUTH

"Come, follow me," Jesus said, "and I will make you fishers of men." At once they left their nets and followed him.

—Matthew 4:19–20

Tribe: A Warrior's Heart

»TRIBAL FACE

John: Fisherman and Apostle

Fishing is John's life. He's barely in his late teens yet he's convinced that throwing nets into the sea and landing the big catch is a good way to make a living. Not only does it put food on his table, but it's also the family thing to do. John and his brother, James, are partners with their father in a prosperous fishing enterprise.

Little does John realize, God has a bigger catch in mind.

One day, while preparing nets as usual with his dad and brother, something amazing happens—an encounter that changes his life forever.

Just off in the distance, not too far away, John spots a man walking along the shore. There's something about His face—a strength matched with gentleness, and something like love that makes him unable to look away. When he speaks, his voice is so compelling.

"Follow me."

That's all He says.

John looks at James with a bewildered expression. James is staring at him too.

With each footprint the man leaves behind in the sand, John's heart beats faster. A unique emotion seems to compel him and his brother to leave the nets.

"Who is that?" John asks. But James is already heading toward the unusual man.

• • •

John and his brother chose to follow Jesus, leaving behind much more than just their nets. They abandoned everything that was familiar to them, every earthly pursuit: money, career, comfort, popularity, pleasure. James and John set off on an amazing adventure that became so much more; unwittingly, they had joined a revolution that was going to change history.

For the next few years, the brothers watched as Jesus healed the sick, brought people back from the grave, and spent endless hours reaching out to the lost and the lonely—those the world would rather have forgotten. James and John lived with the Savior 24/7, walking hundreds of miles with Him, and never once looking back.

If there was anyone who really knew Jesus, these two brothers certainly did. They shared a deep and uncommon connection. The Lord brought them into His inner circle, making them His closest friends—even members of "the big twelve" (the original apostles). These guys were on the mountain with Jesus when God the Father dropped by for a little social time (see Luke 9:28–36).

And John was the only one Jesus asked to look after His mother when He was dying on the cross. What's more, John was the only person Jesus appeared to when He described the end times in the Book of Revelation.

Talk about connected! And this apostle got right down to the point in his book, starting with: "In the beginning was the Word, and the Word was with God, and the Word was God"(John 1:1).

It's not surprising that his account of Jesus' life is one of the most popular books in the Bible. As we read his writings, we can't help but get the idea that John really loved Jesus. His solid faith literally helped to turn the world upside down (actually, more like, right side up). John left behind his old life for something—Someone—much greater.

How about you? Do you want to be set apart, to be a member of the inner circle? There's a place for all of us . . . even salty fishermen.

»TRIBAL TRAINING

• **Know Christ deeper by experiencing Him daily.** Learning about the Lord from a theology textbook is much different from experiencing Him personally in a day-to-day walk. According to the apostle Paul, it's all about faith and fellowship: "I consider everything a loss compared to the surpassing greatness of knowing Christ Jesus my Lord, for whose sake I have lost all things. I consider them rubbish, that I may gain Christ and be found in him, not having a righteousness of my own that comes from the law, but that which is through faith in Christ—the righteousness that comes from God and is by faith." (Philippians 3:8–9).

• **Allow the Lord to realign your priorities.** It's time for a gut check. When it comes to your faith in Christ, where are your priorities? Is having a deeper, stronger attachment to Jesus your number one passion, like it was for John? When you blow it, do you admit it, asking your Savior to renew and transform your heart? What other priorities are filling your heart—friends, girls, entertainment, stuff? Spend some time in prayer, and ask God to take over your priorities.

• **PRAY IT OUT: "Lord, help me to leave behind bland rituals and stale religion so I can follow You in a truly living, exciting way."** Don't just read about faith or settle for secondhand knowledge about Jesus. Ask Him for the strength and courage to give up your old life. Ask Him to show you how to experience Him daily.

» TRIBAL MARKS

A Key Point I Learned Today:

How I Want to Grow:

Heart

Mind

Soul

Prayer List:

Family

Friends

Church

World Issues

»NOTE: This is your space to journal, draw, doodle—whatever you wish! Under the appropriate headings write about your praises, struggles, hopes, dreams. . . and anything else on your mind.

Praise

Battles

Journal

Victories

Adventures

Day 2: Cosmic Communion

»TRIBAL QUEST

Experience communion with your heavenly Father every day, allowing Him to feed your faith and strengthen your spiritual life.

Explore the Word: John 6:41–59

»TRIBAL TRUTH

Jesus said to them, "I tell you the truth, unless you eat the flesh of the Son of Man and drink his blood, you have no life in you. Whoever eats my flesh and drinks my blood has eternal life, and I will raise him up at the last day. For my flesh is real food and my blood is real drink."

—John 6:53–55

»TRIBAL FACE

Neil Armstrong and Buzz Aldrin

July 20, 1969, 4:17 p.m. Eastern Daylight Time. Millions of people on Earth are hearing NASA Mission Commander Neil Armstrong's historic words: "Houston, Tranquility Base here. The Eagle has landed."

No one on Earth outside Mission Control, however, knows what Neil Armstrong and Buzz Aldrin are doing right after landing.

The landing itself took quite some time. Landing the Lunar Module, or LM, was a bit more complicated than turning off the ignition and setting the parking brake. The astronauts had to do about two hours' worth of adjusting valves, programming computers, calculating telemetry, and other chores that prepared the LM to take off again. But once that was completed, they could pay attention to the fact that they were actually on the moon.

Aldrin, a Presbyterian, had brought along a tiny communion set. "This is the LM pilot," he radios to Earth. "I'd like to take this opportunity to ask every person listening in, whoever and wherever they may be, to pause for a moment and contemplate the events of the past few hours and to give thanks in his or her own way."

The communion set has a container of bread, a vial of wine the size of a fingertip, and a miniature silver chalice. Aldrin pours the wine into the chalice, watching with fascination as it slowly curls up the sides of the cup in the moon's weak gravitational pull.

Aldrin reads Jesus' words from John 15:5: "I am the vine; you are the branches. If a man remains in me and I in him, he will bear much fruit; apart from me you can do nothing." Then the astronauts share communion.[1]

• • •

Most of us take communion at church, but can you imagine experiencing it in outer space?

Now imagine something even better: gazing into your heavenly Father's eyes as you take holy communion. That's how it was for Christ's followers.

"Eat My flesh—drink My blood," Jesus told them.

This strange commandment is one of the most important instructions to Christians in the entire Bible. But more than a few people have completely misunderstood it. In fact, some have even accused Christians of being cannibals. What they don't understand is that this symbolic act is the number-one "ingredient" in the life of any believer in Jesus Christ.

Human beings are made up of amino acids, water, minerals, and many other elements. We can't manufacture these ingredients on our own. We need to ingest and absorb them in order to live.

The same is true of our spiritual nature. We cannot manufacture the ingredients we need for our spirits on our own. For spiritual survival, we need spiritual food. And that's what Jesus says He is. We must eat, ingest, and absorb His Spirit into ours. We must digest Him and allow His life to become the sustenance of our spiritual life. If we don't eat His body and drink His blood—that is, make Him a part of us—the only thing waiting for us is spiritual starvation. And with starvation comes death.

His desire is for us to draw so close to Him and love Him so deeply, that He actually becomes a part of us. In that oneness, He will give us overwhelming love, peace, and joy.

And it is that oneness that provides the abundant life He continually promises.[2]

»TRIBAL TRAINING

- **Stop settling for "McFaith."** The "fast-food" spiritual lifestyle provides poor nourishment—a quick prayer here and a Bible verse there is not enough to sustain you in the long run. Instead, sit down to a full meal of prayer, Scripture reading, worship, and fellowship, in an intimate, growing oneness with Jesus. Consider this new level of commitment when you take communion and whenever you recall His promise to strengthen you in your commitment. Make your prayer, *Lord, consume my life.*

- **Commit to having an uninterrupted quiet time every day.** Beginning today, carve out at least 15 minutes of time each day (maybe in the morning or just before going to bed) to seek God through Bible reading and prayer. Also, work to gradually increase the length of your quiet time.

- **Never dine with the devil.** Satan will use every lie he can dream up to convince you that there is no power through Jesus Christ. He wants you to believe that nothing has changed inside you, that you can't have victory over sin. Stop the devil in his tracks by drawing closer to Jesus.

- **PRAY IT OUT: "Lord, give me a hunger for You and feed my soul."** Ask Jesus to give you the true holy communion—oneness with Him that results in overwhelming love, peace, and joy. Ask Him for the authentic abundant life that He promises in Scripture.

»TRIBAL MARKS

A Key Point I Learned Today:

How I Want to Grow:

Heart

Mind

Soul

Prayer List:

Family

Friends

Church

World Issues

Praise

Battles

Journal

Victories

Adventures

Day 3: Wild Truth Encounter

» TRIBAL QUEST

Avoid spiritual blindness, allowing Christ to illuminate the truth.

Explore the Word: Acts 9:1–31

» TRIBAL TRUTH

Immediately, something like scales fell from Saul's eyes, and he could see again.

—Acts 9:18

» TRIBAL FACE

Paul: Missionary and Apostle

A hush falls over the synagogue as a fiery Jew stands before the crowd. Today's speaker: a powerful Pharisee named Saul—the persecutor of the Christians.

It's no secret how Saul feels about Christianity. And everyone knows why he has come to the Roman city of Damascus.

For some time, Saul has been heard breathing murderous threats against the radical members of the Way—the name given to Christ's disciples. Now he is leading a campaign of repression against them, and his Pharisee brothers are excited to bring down the iron fist on their unorthodox teachings.

Saul's eyes scan the synagogue, studying the faces of his fellow Jews and members of the Law. Something about him is different. The words unfold slowly from his lips. "This Man. . . . This Man they call Jesus Christ. . . . He is . . ."

The Jewish leaders look impatient. *Yes, Saul, get on with it. Tell this crowd He was a liar and a fraud. Tell them His followers are a bunch of lunatics and should be behind bars.*

Saul returns their stares. Suddenly, his eyes flicker. "He is . . . truly the Son of God."

A collective gasp rises.

"This Jesus, the One who was dead, is alive! I've seen Him with my own eyes! The Christians are right!"

"This Jesus raised havoc in Jerusalem!" a voice shouts from the crowd.

"Yes! And he has come here to take the Christians as prisoners to the chief priests!" shouts another.

Saul speaks passionately. "This Jesus, I proclaim to you, is the Christ," he says. "If you believe it, you, too, will be saved."

• • •

What happened to this passionate Jew in Damascus? The stern Pharisee, who was once bent on blocking the Way, now burns a path for the Good News of Christ. The feared persecutor, who was once blinded with hate, now sees with a heart focused on love.

When Saul encountered the Christ, he was a new man. A short time later, he received a new name—Paul—and learned three truths about the Messiah: (1) The crucified Jesus actually rose from the dead as the Savior of all people, (2) Though the wages of sin is death, Jesus paid the price with His life, giving us salvation through our acceptance of His sacrifice, and (3) Christians must never be ashamed of the strange-sounding truth of the gospel, but boldly share it with the world—regardless of the opposition.

The Lord gave Paul an important assignment: Tell others about the awesome Good News of Jesus Christ. Flip open your Bible and you'll discover that at least 13 books in the New Testament bear Paul's name. Paul learned to make his mission a priority and place it above everything else: ridicule, abuse, peer pressure, embarrassment . . . even the possibility of losing friends, or even his life.

So, just what can we learn from Paul? How can we fuel our faith—and keep it burning? Take Paul's faith steps. . . .

»TRIBAL TRAINING

Faith Step Number 1: Get your eyes off the world. As I travel around North America speaking or following stories for *Breakaway*, I see the same hassles hounding youth in nearly every city: too many teens haven't learned how to be discerning. They are literally brainwashed by tons of lies from magazines, movies, TV, and their peers at school. The biggest lie teens are swallowing these days goes

something like this: "Hey, what you believe is your thing, and mine is mine.

Wild Truth Encounter

What's right for you may not be right for me." In other words, truth is what you make it. But real Truth is absolute—it doesn't change—and it comes from God. Check out author J. I. Packer's insights on this issue: "We were all created to be God's image-bearers. That means that we were created to seek and find God through seeking and finding the truth about God. We are made in such a way, I believe, that we are only at peace with ourselves when it's God's truth that our minds are grasping and consciously obeying. Human life is lacking dignity until you get to that point."[3]

• **Faith Step Number 2: Desire truth.** Understand that following Christ is not a passing fad. It's a step-by-step *commitment* that involves day-by-day *trust*. Author and contemporary Christian artist Matt Redman explains it this way: "We see only in part, yet what we see is enough to give us hope and purpose on our journey. And as we go about our worship here and now, we keep one eye fixed on the horizon, confident that one day the imperfect will disappear and we shall know fully even as we are fully known."[4]

• **Faith Step Number 3: Choose truth.** Jesus said, "Then you will know the truth, and the truth will set you free" (John 8:32). Are you among the many who have allowed the Truth to set you free? If you could use a Truth recharge, sit down in the quietness of your room (turn off the stereo), and let the invisible God speak the Truth to you through His Word. The Bible isn't only for parents and pastors. The only way you can believe the Truth is to know the Truth. The Scriptures are filled with answers to your most burning questions. Here are just a few:

What should I do when I'm struggling with sin? Romans 6:1–14

Does God really love me? Romans 8:31–39

How can I trust God more? Psalm 37

What is authentic faith, anyhow? Hebrews 11

What is heaven really like? Revelation 21–22

What should I do when I need forgiveness? Psalms 32 and 51

• **PRAY IT OUT: "Lord, open my eyes to the Truth."** Ask Jesus to guard you from being brainwashed by worldly philosophies. Ask Him to illuminate your heart, and then begin to saturate your mind with the Word of God.

»TRIBAL MARKS

A Key Point I Learned Today:

How I Want to Grow:

Heart

Mind

Soul

Prayer List:

Family

Friends

Church

World Issues

Praise

Battles

Journal

Victories

Adventures

Day 4: Empowered by Prayer

»TRIBAL QUEST

Follow your Savior's example by letting prayer empower your life.

Explore the Word: James 5:13–18

»TRIBAL TRUTH

Is any one of you in trouble? He should pray. Is anyone happy? Let him sing songs of praise. Is any one of you sick? He should call the elders of the church to pray over him and anoint him with oil in the name of the Lord. And the prayer offered in faith will make the sick person well; the Lord will raise him up. If he has sinned, he will be forgiven.

—James 5:13–15

»TRIBAL FACE

Constantine: Emperor of Rome

Constantine: powerful warrior, military master—and man of prayer?

As a boy, this promising young Roman was taught by his father, Costantius, to pray to Sol, the unconquerable sun god who, as he described, "is creator of all things."

Many years passed, and by A.D. 312, Constantine—now the ruler over the western half of the Roman Empire—is a man who hungers to know his true Creator. During a journey to Rome, as his troops take a midday break, Constantine slips away to his tent for a time of reflection and prayer.

"Reveal to me who You are, Your true nature," he cries to God. "And stretch forth Your right hand to help me in these coming difficulties."

Then, the miraculous happens.

Right in the middle of his prayers, Constantine is interrupted by soldiers shouting outside his tent. One of his servants frantically enters and asks him to follow him outside. When the stern military leader emerges, he sees his troops gazing upward and pointing. He follows their gaze and is equally awestruck by the sight in the sky. Shining brighter than the afternoon sun is a cross with the inscription beneath it, "In This Sign, Conquer." Constantine later realizes that it's not the "unconquerable sun" that has answered his prayer, but the "Unconquerable Son."[5]

Tribe: A Warrior's Heart

Constantine again retires to his tent, pondering the meaning of this vision. That evening when he drifts off to sleep, he dreams that Jesus Christ Himself visits him with a message: "Make a likeness of this sign, which you also saw in the heavens, and it will be a protection in all of your confrontations with your enemies."

Overjoyed by these experiences, the symbol of the cross and the name of Christ are, from then on, carried before the armies of Rome. And on October 28, 312 A.D., a power struggle erupts between Constantine and his fiercest enemy—the ruler of the eastern half of the Roman Empire, a ruthless titan named Maxentius. Their armies face off at the Milvian Bridge outside of Rome. Constantine, as he later tells the historian Eusebius, turns to the Christian God for help—and wins a decisive battle. This secures his place as the Roman emperor.

Constantine now openly embraces Christianity and puts an end to the relentless persecution of Christ's followers. He abolishes crucifixions and ends gladiatorial contests as punishments. He even issues the Edict of Milan, which says, in essence, "Everyone who has a common wish to follow the religion of Christianity may from this moment freely proceed without annoyance." What's more, he establishes Sunday as a holiday, builds churches, finances Christian projects, and gathers bishops and others who know the Christian doctrines and makes them his advisors.

This military-leader-turned-theologian spends the rest of his reign immersed in daily prayer, as well as the study of the Holy Scriptures—always hungering for a deeper knowledge of God.

• • •

Happy ending, right? A true testimony of a transformed life—and the power of prayer. Well—not exactly. Constantine didn't have an apostle Paul-style conversion (as we read about on Day 3). According to some theologians, it took this military leader a bit longer to get his heart right with God. Some even claim that it didn't truly happen until he was on his death bed.

While everything looked good on the surface, appearances can be deceiving. The truth is, Constantine was dedicated to Jesus because of what Christ *did for him*. But when it came to issues such as morality, obedience to the Scriptures, genuine prayer, and personal sacrifice for his faith, Constantine did whatever he wanted—he was, after all, the emperor. Under his reign, Christianity went from being a persecuted religion to being the fashionable way of life. A trend was started that still poses a challenge to believers today:

cultural Christianity. Instead of seeking Jesus with pure hearts and allowing Him to transform their lives, many Christians during Constantine's rule lived their faith only as an outward display for others to see.[6]

Warning: Jesus does not tolerate this kind of behavior. He knows our motives and wants an authentic relationship with us. And when it comes to prayer, our hearts must be sincere. James tells us that the effectual, fervent prayer of a righteous man accomplishes much.

Do you come humbly before the Lord and pray with pure motives? Are you committed to real prayer?

»TRIBAL TRAINING

• **Enter into God's presence through prayer.** Imagine that—the Creator connects with His creation through prayer! The Lord governs both world events and our individual lives, and He is always ready to act and to intervene for our good, His glory, and the progress of the gospel. He longs to demonstrate His power in the tremendous trials that shake the foundation of our lives, as well as in the tiny troubles that merely annoy us. Giant needs are never too great for His power; small ones are never too insignificant for His love. So, don't hold back. Share your heart in prayer—your dreams and desires, your fears, your frustrations, everything! Talk to Jesus just like you would talk to your best friend. (Actually, He *is* your best Friend!)

• **Understand the purpose of prayer.** It's designed to get you on track with God's will, not to adjust *Him* to your agenda. Here's how author Henry T. Blackaby explains it: "Prayer does not give you spiritual power. Prayer aligns your life with God so that He chooses to demonstrate His power through you. The purpose of prayer is not to convince God to change your circumstances but to prepare you to be involved in God's activity."[7]

Prayer is on God's terms, according to His will, and in His perfect timing. So, if you've prayed and prayed without seeing the results you had hoped for, maybe God has something else in mind. Refocus your prayers on what God wants to see happen in you.

• **Expect results when you pray.** Not only are we called to this divine activity (see Philippians 4:6 and 1 Timothy 2:1–3), we are guaranteed of God's action in response to our prayers. As 2 Chronicles points out, if we pray, God promises results.

• **PRAY IT OUT: "Lord, give me a passion for prayer—and give me the words when I don't know how to pray."** Ask Jesus to reveal Himself to you through prayer. Ask Him to open your hands and your heart, so you can receive His many blessings.

»TRIBAL MARKS

A Key Point I Learned Today:

How I Want to Grow:

Heart

Mind

Soul

Prayer List:

Family

Friends

Church

World Issues

Empowered by Prayer

Praise

Battles

Journal

Victories

Adventures

Day 5: Living God's Word

» TRIBAL QUEST

Let God's Word illuminate your path, leading you from darkness to eternal life.

Explore the Word: 2 Timothy 3:10–17

» TRIBAL TRUTH

All Scripture is God-breathed and is useful for teaching, rebuking, correcting and training in righteousness, so that the man of God may be thoroughly equipped for every good work.

—2 Timothy 3:16–17

» TRIBAL FACE

Floyd Cox: West Virginian Coal Miner

Deep. Dark. Dusty.

It's the eerie, alien world of a West Virginia coal mine. Your heart pounds as you descend into the blackness—with nothing but a headlamp to light your steps. Breathing is a challenge, and a fine layer of coal dust sticks to every inch of your body.

You pause to catch your breath. The stuffy air and damp, musty smells are ominous reminders: You are literally *inside* the earth.

But the men who work the mines don't come here for the views (or lack

of them). They do it out of loyalty—commitment to their families, communities, and friends. They do it to earn a paycheck and to carve out a life *above* the ground.

Floyd Cox is one of those brave men.

In the tiny mountain town of Pineville, West Virginia, the abundant seams of coal ripple through the landscape. These ancient deposits are his treasure. Coal heats his house and puts food on the table for him, his wife, and his three daughters.

"Coal is valuable, but it's not the *real* treasure of life," he is fond of saying. He tells this to everyone—from burly miners to the busloads of kids he drives to church on Sunday mornings. "It's not even nearly the most valuable."

He holds up his Bible. "This is the true treasure."

Floyd is a man who *lives* God's Word. He trusts it, reveres it, and is never ashamed to talk about it. As it did for the Psalmist, the Scriptures illuminate his path brighter than the headlamp on the hardhat that he wears.

Through the many long years, this West Virginian has learned a secret from the mines—based in Scripture: Only Jesus Christ can provide the "coal" for your soul and lead you from darkness into the light of eternal life.

● ● ●

Of all the faith heroes I've written about in this book, Floyd is the one I most want to be like.

If you happen to drive through Pineville, you won't see billboards with his photo on them or statues erected in his honor. But if you mention his name, you'll bring smiles to a lot of people's faces. Those who know Floyd see more than a hard-working coal miner. They see a follower of Christ. They see a man who walks, talks, and *lives* God's Word.

"You yourselves are our letter, written on our hearts, known and read by everybody. You show that you are a letter from Christ, the result of our ministry, written not with ink but with the Spirit of the living God, not on tablets of stone but on tablets of human hearts" (2 Corinthians 3:2–3).

This is how Jesus wants us to be. He wants our very lives to read like a letter from heaven—"known and read by everybody."

God's Word is relevant and absolutely accurate in everything He felt was essential for us to know. Scripture is "God-breathed" and offers solid advice for just about every situation you'll ever encounter. Through the Bible, God teaches, rebukes, corrects, and trains us in righteousness. These ancient words are amazingly timeless.

Living God's Word

Without the Bible, we wouldn't know: (1) what God is like, (2) His plan for humans like you and me, (3) how much He loves us, (4) the right way to live on this planet, or (5) anything about what will happen to us after death.

Like Floyd, do you hunger for God's Word, and do you live it—or have you lost your appetite? How can you make Bible study a more meaningful experience? How can you lose your anxieties about exploring God's Word?

»TRIBAL TRAINING

• Clue in to how the Bible is organized. Let's accept the obvious: The Holy Bible is a big thick book with tiny print and very few pictures. But instead of feeling intimidated, make an effort to get the most out of Scripture. It isn't just one book. It's actually a library of 66 books, or booklets, bound into a single volume! Also, the Bible is divided into two primary collections of books. For more, turn to "SURVIVOR STUFF #1: Tribal Treasure Map (How the Bible Is Organized)" on page 183.

• Clue into meaningful Bible study. Try this plan:

Read Scripture with a prayerful heart. Ask God to minister to you through His Word. If you sit down to read and your heart is not prepared, you can miss a message God has just for you.

Establish a daily Bible study plan. Reading a chapter at a time is always a good way to start, but the issue is not how much you get through. Instead, make it a goal to understand what you've read and to find ways of applying it to your life. For an awesome way to read the Bible in a year, turn to "SURVIVOR STUFF #2: Tribal-Truth-in-a-Year Reading Plan" on page 185.

Commit Scripture to memory. In addition to reading the Bible, get in the habit of memorizing verses. The more Scripture you get in your head, the stronger you'll grow spiritually.

Ask yourself questions: "Is there a sin I need to confess? Is there a promise I need to claim? Is there an attitude I need to change? Is there a commitment I need to make? Is there an example I need to follow?"

• PRAY IT OUT: "Lord, help me to live Your Word." Ask God to give you a hunger for the Bible. Ask Him to show you how to be a better witness.

»TRIBAL MARKS

A Key Point I Learned Today:

How I Want to Grow:

Heart

Mind

Soul

Prayer List:

Family

Friends

Church

World Issues

Living God's Word

Praise

Battles

Journal

Victories

Adventures

OBEDIENCE

Day 6: Obedience in the Fangs of Danger

» TRIBAL QUEST

Commit your heart to obeying God—following His commands out of genuine love, not legalistic duty.

Explore the Word: Daniel 6:1–28

» TRIBAL TRUTH

"My God sent his angel, and he shut the mouths of the lions. They have not hurt me, because I was found innocent in his sight."

—Daniel 6:22

» TRIBAL FACE

Daniel: Governor of Babylon

Daniel knows what obedience to God requires.

Radical, unwavering submission to the one, true King—even at the cost of losing popularity, prestige, position. Even in the fangs of danger.

Daniel knows this degree of obedience, and despite the order not to pray, he stays committed to his God. After all, he's seen the Master's hand move in amazing ways—especially the time when three fellow believers were thrown into a blazing furnace.

The flames were kind of hot. King Nebuchadnezzar's soldiers died by simply getting too near as they threw Shadrach, Meshach, and Abednego into the massive furnace. Yet the three men of God with the unfortunate names stayed in there for a while and eventually stepped out unharmed. The account in Daniel 4 says that not a single hair on their heads was singed!

"Praise be to the God of Shadrach, Meshach, and Abednego," the king proclaimed. "They trusted in Him and defied the king's command and were willing to give up their lives rather than serve or worship any god except their own God."

Now, many years later, the opposition to God and His people continues. Babylon's administrators have convinced the new puppet king, Darius the Mede, to issue a decree banning prayer.

Daniel doesn't falter. He kneels at his upstairs window—the one opened toward Jerusalem—and prays in the way he always has, three times a day, giving thanks to God, just as before.

The trap set, the administrators find Daniel praying and return to the king. "Did you not publish a decree? Daniel pays no attention."
Though Darius is "deeply distressed" about punishing Daniel on whom he had previously relied for wisdom, the administrators make a solid case, and Daniel is thrown to the lions.

"May your God, whom you serve continually, rescue you," the king tells Daniel. Then a stone is placed over the entrance to the lion's den.

Daniel's life should have ended right there. Yet, as in the furnace, God sends His protection and rescues His obedient child.

The following morning, Darius finds Daniel unscratched, and after ordering the administrators themselves thrown into the lion's den, he issues a new decree: "that in every part of my kingdom people must fear and reverence the God of Daniel. For he is the living God and he endures forever; his kingdom will not be destroyed, his dominion will never end. He rescues and he saves; he performs signs and wonders in the heavens and on the earth. He has rescued Daniel from the power of the lions" (Daniel 6:26–27).

• • •

Radical obedience in the fangs of danger. Unwavering submission to the King of kings. That's how Daniel lived his faith. He didn't know exactly what would happen to him in the pit, but he did know this: God is God, the One and Only, and He can be trusted—even when starving lions are poised to pounce.

Hopefully you'll never have to prove your faith against the fangs of hungry beasts or in the belly of a fiery furnace. But regardless, you encounter choices every day that test your beliefs—the temptation to lie (or "bend the truth"), a struggle with lust (or "just a peek"), curiosity about drugs and alcohol (or "just experimenting").

How do you choose? Which decisions will honor God and speak boldly of your radical obedience?

»TRIBAL TRAINING

• **Count the cost.** How expensive is living for Christ? It has cost many men and women everything—including their lives. The grace God offers us cost Christ everything—including His life. Accepting it and living for Him is the most expensive decision anyone can make (especially in areas like

trust, commitment, and total obedience). The choice is yours. Will you follow the crowd and conform to the world, or, like Daniel, commit yourself to standing strong for God (and leading others in the same direction)? It all starts with the first step: the desire to follow Christ.

Take a look at what Christian scholar Dietrich Bonhoeffer said: "Costly grace is the gospel . . . the gift that must be asked for, the door at which a man must knock. Such grace is costly because it calls us to follow. . . . It is costly because it costs a man his life . . . because it condemns sin . . . what has cost God much cannot be cheap for us."[8]

• **Do business with the Lord without delay.** Your strength and resolve to radical obedience comes from God—in every area of your life. While the cost is high, the rewards are immeasurable. All it takes is your willingness to be aligned with His will: "This is the confidence we have in approaching God: that if we ask anything according to his will, he hears us. And if we know that he hears us—whatever we ask—we know that we have what we asked of him" (1 John 5:14–15).

• **PRAY IT OUT: "Lord, teach me to be obedient."** Ask Jesus to give you strength when you are weak, courage when you are tempted, and trust when you doubt. Ask Him to give you a heart that seeks His pleasure.

»TRIBAL MARKS

A Key Point I Learned Today:

How I Want to Grow:

Heart

Mind

Soul

Prayer List:

Family

Friends

Church

World Issues

Praise

Battles

Journal

Victories

Adventures

Day 7: With Tongues Like Fire

»TRIBAL QUEST

Be tuned in to the Holy Spirit for discernment, for guidance, and for the strength to be Christ's witness.

Explore the Word: Acts 2:1–21

»TRIBAL TRUTH

When the day of Pentecost came, they were all together in one place. Suddenly a sound like the blowing of a violent wind came from heaven and filled the whole house where they were sitting. They saw what seemed to be tongues of fire that separated and came to rest on each of them. All of them were filled with the Holy Spirit and began to speak in other tongues as the Spirit enabled them.

—Acts 2:1–4

»TRIBAL FACE

Simon Peter: Fisherman and Apostle

Andrew is stunned by what he sees. He blinks a few times and refocuses. "It just can't be! Is this really happening?"

Right there in the crowed room on Jerusalem's Upper Street, he and the other disciples are encountering something supernatural. It begins with a sound like a violent wind. Then Andrew glances at his brother, Simon Peter, and sees something like a tongue of fire coming down on his head. And Simon begins speaking passionately, but in a language Andrew has never heard before.

Suddenly, the roar of the wind is not a sound anymore; it's a storm within his own soul, and Andrew is filled to bursting. He opens his mouth and begins to speak as enthusiastically as Simon, but in a different language altogether.

All the disciples have tongues of flame resting upon them. And all are speaking various languages. Foreign Jews who heard them yelling in their own foreign tongues have arrived to witness it. This is the Holy Spirit! Yes, this is power from on high, the promise of Jesus, and that's what Simon has been bellowing about.

Andrew's whole being "sings with the breathing of God."[9]

When some people standing on the steps outside begin to make fun of them, saying that they're drunk, Peter shouts, "No! We are not drunk!" His booming voice silences the crowd. "You are witnessing what Joel prophesied long ago: God is pouring out His Spirit! As Joel said, 'In the last days, your sons and daughters will prophesy, your young men will see visions, your old men will dream dreams. Even on My servants, both men and women, I will pour out My Spirit in those days, and they will prophesy.'"

"Listen to me," Simon Peter calls. "What you see and hear today—this is the work of Jesus! Repent and be baptized, every one of you, in the name of Jesus Christ for the forgiveness of your sins. And you will receive the gift of the Holy Spirit. The promise is for you and your children and for all who are far off—for all whom the Lord our God will call."

• • •

Imagine being one of the disciples on that day. What would it have been like to feel that power surging through your body? It was probably the greatest feeling in the world!

What Peter shouted to the masses is true. If you've committed your heart to Jesus, then you share this experience, this supernatural, eternal "gift."

The Holy Spirit—the third Person of the Trinity—is our Guide, our Helper, our Strengthener, and our Advocate, sent to live in us and to control every aspect of our lives. Like the Father and the Son, God the Holy Spirit is to be believed and obeyed.

The first thing the Spirit will prompt you to do is speak about Jesus to others.

Empowered by the Holy Spirit, Peter took his heavenly assignment to heart. He stood before the Sanhedrin, the very men who would soon murder Stephen. It was Peter who later took the message of salvation to the Gentiles. Peter was the man whom King Herod imprisoned for his refusal to stop preaching the Good News, and then was miraculously freed by an angel. And it was Peter whose death, Jesus said, would "glorify God" (John 21:19).[10]

God sent the Holy Spirit to fill our hearts, so that we might sense His presence in our lives. Can you hear His voice directing your steps? Are you, like Peter, stepping out with power as Christ's witness?

»TRIBAL TRAINING

- **Be guided.** The Holy Spirit is a Counselor who lives in and with and all around us. Through His guidance, you can fulfill all the goals and plans God has for you. Call on the Holy Spirit for guidance in understanding God's message to you here and elsewhere in your life.

- **Be encouraged.** The Spirit takes away fear—of rejection, of change, of failure—and gives hope and courage to face life's challenges. Jesus said, "You will receive power when the Holy Spirit comes on you; and you will be my witnesses" (Acts 1:8).

- **Be comforted.** In times of trouble—when things seem too hard to handle—it is the Holy Spirit who is there to help you. Trust Him and know that He is your comfort and peace.

- **PRAY IT OUT: "Lord, fill me with the Holy Spirit."** Ask Him to draw you into His inner circle, helping you to know Him better. Ask the Lord to give you guidance and wisdom during times of turmoil and times of tranquility—during moments that involve big decisions and small ones.

»TRIBAL MARKS

A Key Point I Learned Today:

How I Want to Grow:

Heart

Mind

Soul

Prayer List:

Family

Friends

Church

World Issues

With Tongues Like Fire

Praise

Battles

Tribe: A Warrior's Heart

Journal

Victories

Adventures

Living Without
Secrets

Day 8: The Sin Solution

» TRIBAL QUEST

Vow to not let sin reign in your body or become your master.

Explore the Word: Mark 1:40–42 and Romans 6:8–14

» TRIBAL TRUTH

A man with leprosy came to him and begged him on his knees, "If you are willing, you can make me clean." Filled with compassion, Jesus reached out his hand and touched the man. "I am willing," he said. "Be clean!" Immediately the leprosy left him and he was cured.

—Mark 1:40–42

» TRIBAL FACE

Leper Outcast Healed by Jesus

Broken. Lonely. Desperate.

The outcast spends his life on the fringes, and his days are lived in the shadows. But news travels quickly throughout Galilee—even on these forgotten back roads.

The man knows he doesn't have a minute to waste. This is his only hope. He must reach the center of town. Not making it there means inevitable destruction. The eternal end to an already pitiful life.

The man covers his hideous physique in his pungent wrap and steps out of a dark alley. Suddenly, a scream pierces the air. The man peeks out from behind his hood and watches as a woman grabs her child and races to the other side of the street.

"Don't come around here!" yells a person on his right.

"Stay away!" screams another. "You know you're not welcome!"

"Get away from us, unclean one—you LEPER!"

Everywhere he goes, the man is treated like garbage. But it doesn't stop him. He ignores the biting words and continues to hobble along the hot, dusty road—eventually reaching a crowd at the end of the street.

Standing among the people is the only Man who won't reject him; the one Man who has the power to make him well. A Nazarene. A carpenter. God in the flesh, speaking to the broken and lonely, the desperate and diseased.

And when he reaches Jesus, the most incredible thing happens. The leper falls on his knees and begs, "If You are willing, You can make me clean." Seeing the man's faith, Jesus is filled with compassion and reaches out His hand to touch the man. "I am willing," He says. "Be clean!" And immediately the man is cured.

• • •

Amazing story. To me, it's one of the greatest in the Bible.

I know what you're thinking: *But the Bible has way better stories than this! Like Jesus walking on water, or Moses parting the Red Sea, or Jonah being swallowed by a whale . . . What's so amazing about this one?*

Well, the leper wasn't just some no-name person who got a second chance at life. This guy is just like you and me. Now hold on. He had a repulsive, deadly disease—just like the sin that plagues us all. Oh, sure, we may not have festering sores on the outside, but inside, we all have them.

Each of us has a condition that's every bit as bad, if not worse, than leprosy. It's deadly, and it kills both body and soul.

When the Great Physician reached out His hand and said, "I am willing," He was also talking to you and me.

When that pitiful, struggling, dying man made his way to see the Holy One, and said, "You can make me clean," how did Jesus respond? Was He grossed out? Did He spit on the man and order him to get lost? Did He turn away and gag?

Jesus did what only a Savior would do. He stretched out His hand and healed.

He also stretches out His hand to you and me today. He loves us in spite of our sin. He wants to forgive us and cure us of our deadly disease—the disease of sin.

"I am willing," He says. "Are you?"

The Sin Solution

» TRIBAL TRAINING

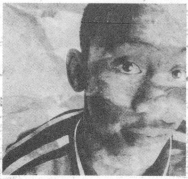

- **Face the sin struggle.** Be honest: You've committed your life to Christ, but your old nature still exists. And if you encourage it, it can literally take control. The result: a strained relationship with God. It's as if there's a tug-of-war going on inside of you. You want to do what's right, you want to please God, yet you find yourself giving in to temptation. Even one of the great heroes of the faith, the apostle Paul, agonized with this same problem: "I do not understand what I do. For what I want to do I do not do, but what I hate I do. . . . For I have the desire to do what is good, but I cannot carry it out" (Romans 7:15, 18).

- **Confess your mistakes immediately.** This is the key to winning the tug-of-war against sin. It's the answer to making things right again, and preventing your old nature from ruining your new life in Christ. You don't have to live with a huge load of guilt and shame. Tell Jesus all about your sins, tell Him how sorry you are. He will forgive you: "If we confess our sins, he is faithful and just and will forgive us our sins and purify us from all unrighteousness" (1 John 1:9).

- **Know that the Lord won't give up on you** — even if it's the same sin you confessed yesterday. When you're truly seeking after Jesus, no sin can keep you from Him. You'll find acceptance, love, and freedom — despite your shortcomings. Ask Him to go deep into your heart and to heal the real cause of what's making you stumble.

- **Strive to follow a new path.** Once you've confessed the sin and asked Jesus to help you change, stop flogging yourself. You're totally forgiven. With your relationship restored, seek your new path (with help from the Holy Spirit).

- **Take up your shield.** Make it a goal to memorize Romans 6:12–14. Then, when you're tempted, use these words as your shield: "I will not let sin reign in my body. I will not offer my body as an instrument of wickedness. Sin is not my master. I'm under grace. Jesus is my Lord."

- **PRAY IT OUT: "Lord, cleanse the sin from my heart and make me the man You want me to be."** Ask for Jesus' help to overcome your weaknesses and to steer you clear of temptation.

Tribe: A Warrior's Heart

»TRIBAL MARKS

A Key Point I Learned Today:

How I Want to Grow:

Heart

Mind

Soul

Prayer List:

Family

Friends

Church

World Issues

Praise

Battles

Journal

Victories

Adventures

Day 9: Hearts Set Ablaze

HEARTS SET ABLAZE

»TRIBAL QUEST

Spend time in serious reflection, identifying idols and roadblocks to faith.
Explore the Word: 1 John 5:1–21

»TRIBAL TRUTH

We know that anyone born of God does not continue to sin; the one who was born of God keeps him safe, and the evil one cannot harm him. We know that we are children of God, and that the whole world is under the control of the evil one. We know also that the Son of God has come and has given us understanding, so that we may know him who is true. And we are in him who is true—even in his Son Jesus Christ. He is the true God and eternal life. Dear children, keep yourselves from idols.

—1 John 5:18–21

»TRIBAL FACE

John Wesley: Scholar and Evangelist

"Catch on fire, and people will come for miles to watch you burn."

Blunt words that shock the ears, yet to John Wesley it's the only way to

experience life with Christ.

John is an Oxford scholar who crisscrosses England (ultimately traveling 250,000 miles throughout his lifetime), speaking with fire and passion about the gospel. The open air is his sanctuary, and everywhere this minister goes—from factory yards to town squares—he draws a crowd. His mission: Wake up a sleepy church.

"God is continually saying to every child of man: 'My son, give Me thy heart!' And to give our hearts to any other is plain idolatry. Accordingly, whatever takes our heart from Him, or shares it with Him, is an idol."

John knows this from experience. His own heart was caught up in idolatry—even after identifying himself with Christ. Eventually, it was "strangely warmed" and revived.

But that didn't occur until after his brush with death.

The year is 1738, and John is sailing home to England after an unsuccessful missionary trip to the colony of Georgia. He had hoped to convert the Indians to Christ but was ineffective. What's more, he can't help feeling that something is desperately missing from his faith. "I went to America to convert the Indians, but, oh, who shall convert me?" he later wrote.[11]

How well John remembers the trip two years earlier to America:

He was feeling very small against the endless ocean and infinite sky, when suddenly, BOOM! There was a thunderclap and a bolt of lightning. Then a few chilly droplets, followed by an all-out downpour.

Before long, mountainous waves rose around the tiny ship, jetting it toward the clouds, then plunging it deep into churning canyons. Violent swells moved in like a band of ruthless pirates, turning the once peaceful waters of the Atlantic into dangerous thieves.

John panicked as he watched the waves rise and fall. He headed below deck and began to pray: "O God in heaven, I fear we may not make it. I fear this may be the end. But I'm not ready to die. In fact, I fear death."

John looked up, and his eyes focused on a curious group of passengers—members of a religious order called the Moravian Brethren. Despite the chaos outside, these people were calm and projected an amazing inner peace.

I must have what they've found, John vowed silently.

Several weeks later, with the nightmare at sea behind him, John visited a Moravian Society meeting held at Nettleton Court in England. At last, he discovered what was missing in his life: complete trust in Jesus Christ as his Lord and Savior; the assurance of the forgiveness of his sins and eternal life in heaven.

Right there in that tiny building—after years spent pursuing religion instead of relationship—he finally came to know the experience of genuine conversion. His heart was set ablaze by the one, true Living God. In his journal, he wrote:

> *In the evening I went very unwillingly to a society in Aldersgate Street, where one was reading Luther's preface to the Epistle to the Romans. About a quarter before nine, while he was describing the change, which God works in the heart through faith in Christ, I felt my heart strangely warmed. I felt I did trust in Christ, Christ alone, for my salvation; and an assurance was given me that He had taken away my sins, even mine, and saved me from the law of sin and death.*[12]

• • •

As a young man, John Wesley hungered to know God intimately. Raised in a Christian home, he committed himself to prayer and Bible study, yearning to "draw ever closer to Jesus." Yet despite his good intentions, like many in the same circumstances, he left out one crucial element of faith: relationship.

For much of his early Christian walk, John was more concerned about following "spiritual rules" and attaining head knowledge. What's more, he hadn't given Jesus total control of his life. Instead, he allowed his heart to be filled with idols: other people as well as his own pride, reputation, and accomplishments—his will versus God's will.

Did you realize that? An idol can be a person, a pursuit—anything that takes priority over Jesus. And if we don't let the Lord call the shots in our lives, we can end up living like an idolater—without even realizing it.

"I am not being flippant when I say that all of us suffer from addiction," says expert Gerald G. May, M.D. "Nor am I reducing the meaning of addiction. I mean in all truth that the psychological, neurological, and spiritual dynamics of full-fledged addiction are actively at work in every human being. The same processes that are responsible for addiction to alcohol and narcotics are also responsible for addiction to ideas, work, relationships, power, moods, fantasies, and an endless variety of other things. We are all addicts in every sense of the word."

Dr. May says our addictions are our own worst enemies. They enslave us with chains of our own making, and yet they are beyond our control. "Addiction also makes idolaters of us all because it forces us to worship these objects of attachment, thereby preventing us from truly, freely loving

God and one another. . . . Yet, in still another paradox, our addictions can lead us to a deep appreciation of grace. They can bring us to our knees."[13]

What idols rule your life? What are your addictions? Are you surrendering all to Christ? Do you yearn for a greater level of spiritual intimacy with Jesus—a heart set ablaze?

»TRIBAL TRAINING

• **Don't live in denial.** As John Wesley warned, Christians aren't immune to idolatry. And as Dr. May points out, all of us suffer from addictions. Perhaps money or materialism is your idol. Maybe you're addicted to a relationship, or you hunger for approval and acceptance—or may you hold secret addictions drugs or lust.

• **Evaluate yourself.** (1) Ask questions: *What are my addictions? Are these idols in my life? Do others notice my attachment to these things? Am I willing to accept the truth about them? Do I want to surrender them to Jesus? Do I believe He is able to help me overcome my misplaced desires?* (2) List every addiction and idol you have in the space below, along with your thoughts, fears, and prayers about them.

• **Evaluate your faith.** Are your affections "nailed" to something or someone other than God? When things get bad, do you put your trust in the Savior or do you retreat to other so-called "safe places"—the arms of a girlfriend, or another, less than holy source of power? Does your walk with Christ feel hindered?

• **Seek counsel.** Whether it's a parent, a coach, a pastor, or a therapist, find a wise person you can trust. I've said it before, and I will say it again: Find a partner to whom you can be accountable.

• **PRAY IT OUT: "Lord, tear down the idols in my life, crush the addictions, rip out the roadblocks—and set my heart on fire for You."** Pull off your masks, uncover your secrets, and pour out your heart to Jesus. Don't hold back—confess everything. Ask the Holy Spirit for the answers. Then be willing to listen and trust.

»TRIBAL MARKS

A Key Point I Learned Today:

How I Want to Grow:

Heart

Mind

Soul

Prayer List:

Family

Friends

Church

World Issues

Journal

Praise

Battles

Victories

Adventures

Day 10: Strength for the Climb

» TRIBAL QUEST

When your struggles seem too big to face and the climb feels too tough to endure, lean on Christ for strength.

Explore the Word: Psalm 121

» TRIBAL TRUTH

I lift up my eyes to the hills—where does my help come from? My help comes from the LORD, the Maker of heaven and earth.

—Psalm 121:1–2

» TRIBAL FACE

Todd Huston: Adventurer and Mountain Climber

Todd Huston swallows hard as he faces his mountain. Today it's McKinley—the highest point in North America. Yesterday it was learning to live with a disability.

If he reaches the summit of the peak, he'll rank among the few elite climbers who have conquered this giant. Even more impressive, he'll have done it on a prosthetic leg—making him a conqueror of an even bigger mountain.

After resting at the top of a ridge, Todd continues his ascent up an extremely icy slope called Pig Hill. Everything he'd heard about the killer climb reinforces his fears—crevasses, glaciers, sheer ice walls, violent storms, plummeting temperatures, whiteouts. But this slope will determine his fate, pushing him beyond anything he'd imagined during his months of intense training. This wicked wall threatens to break him.

The rest is easy, he tells himself silently. *Get past Pig Hill. The rest is easy.*

But with each step, a fresh spasm of pain explodes in his boot and sears the end of his stump—step after step. This is the most grueling climb of all, and it's taking its toll on his body. His lungs threaten to burst with every breath. His heartbeat drums against his temples to the rhythm of his pain.

Just when he is at the point of giving up, his climbing partner points. "There it is—the summit!"

Todd gazes in awe. The summit seems unconquerable. *We still have to go that much farther?*

But from Pig Hill, it's an easy trek. Whether it's the gradual ascent or the adrenaline subduing his excitement, Todd maintains a slow but steady pace along the ridge at 20,000 feet. Up ahead, another climber raises his hands in triumph. He has reached the summit.

Todd accelerates his pace and lunges the last few feet. His eyes catch sight of several flags left by previous expeditions.

"Thank God!" he shouts and his voice fills every crevasse and canyon in Denali National Park.[14]

• • •

After the McKinley expedition, Todd explained to a reporter: "I see myself as a representative of the 43 million Americans who, on any given day, are struggling against a major illness, a disability, or any other health-related challenge." He went on to describe challenges that wouldn't show up on any doctor's X-ray—divorce, death of a loved one, or overcoming drug and alcohol addiction.

Todd's physical challenges began during his teen years. At age 14, a water skiing accident severed his right leg. Amazingly, doctors saved the limb and reattached it. But several weeks later, infection set in. And after enduring 28 surgeries and grueling physical therapy, this young man from Tulsa, Oklahoma, had to face the possibility of losing his leg.

"I tried to hide my physical scars from my friends," he explains. "I seldom swam, and I used humor to hide the mental scars. But what hurt most was not being able to play football. That sport had been my life. As a middle linebacker during seventh and eighth grade, I held the record at Byrd Junior High for the most tackles."

Questions about God and his relationship with Jesus swirled around his head. One day, while sitting in a park beneath a tree, he opened his Bible and began reading the Psalms. Then, he struggled to his feet and looked up through the branches and leaves into the sky. "Lord, I'm Yours," he prayed aloud.

With Todd's soul now right with God, he knew it was time to have a healthy body, too. Letting his doctor amputate a portion of his right leg just below his knee was the only solution. A gentle rush of God's power filled him with peace and the knowledge that Jesus would see him through the challenges ahead. But never in his wildest dreams did Todd imagine that he'd one day stand on one of North America's highest peaks.

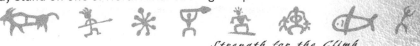

"I had climbed my mountains and seen the other side," he explains. "I had dodged thunderstorms, battled blizzards, endured incredible pain, and faced my fears through faith in God. I had gained a deeper experience with Him. Time after time, when it seemed the expedition was doomed, He smoothed the way. Time after time, when my body hurt so badly that I thought I couldn't take another step, He infused me with the strength to continue. Time after time, He was there. Now I know He always will be."

How's your climb with God? Are struggles and challenges getting the best of you? Don't lose hope. Call out to Christ. He'll give you the strength to persevere.

TRIBAL TRAINING

» • **Realize that struggle is a part of life.** A friend once said to me, "Dead things don't struggle!" Good observation.

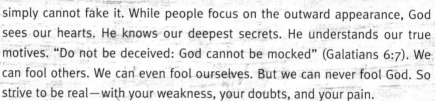

• **Trust that God has not abandoned you.** In times of distress, lean on Him. Jesus will give you the power of the Holy Spirit. He will help you handle whatever it is that you must face.

• **Never hide behind a mask.** When it comes to our relationship with God, we simply cannot fake it. While people focus on the outward appearance, God sees our hearts. He knows our deepest secrets. He understands our true motives. "Do not be deceived: God cannot be mocked" (Galatians 6:7). We can fool others. We can even fool ourselves. But we can never fool God. So strive to be real—with your weakness, your doubts, and your pain.

• **Hold on to hope.** Remind yourself of these truths when the going gets rough:

"Again Jesus said, 'Peace be with you! As the Father has sent me, I am sending you.' And with that he breathed on them and said, 'Receive the Holy Spirit'" (John 20:21–22).

"This is love for God: to obey his commands. And his commands are not burdensome, for everyone born of God overcomes the world" (1 John 5:3–4).

• **PRAY IT OUT: "Lord, help me handle what seems impossible."** Cry out to Jesus when life's challenges seem too hard to endure. Ask Him to give you hope and restore joy in your heart.

»TRIBAL MARKS

A Key Point I Learned Today:

How I Want to Grow:

Heart

Mind

Soul

Prayer List:

Family

Friends

Church

World Issues

Strength for the Climb

Praise

Battles

Journal

Victories

Adventures

THOUGHT LIFE

Day 11: Your Private Thought Life

»TRIBAL QUEST

Choose a life of holiness, never allowing pride or lust to be your downfall.

Explore the Word: Judges 16:1–22

»TRIBAL TRUTH

Some time later, he fell in love with a woman in the Valley of Sorek whose name was Delilah. The rulers of the Philistines went to her and said, "See if you can lure him into showing you the secret of his great strength and how we can overpower him so we may tie him up and subdue him."

—*Judges 16:4–5*

»TRIBAL FACE

Samson: Nazirite Strongman and Protector of Israel

Delilah—her name sounds like *layla,* the Hebrew word for "night," making her seem all the more mysterious, all the more enticing to a man who loves women, especially foreign women. Samson strokes her hair and then cups her delicate face in his hands, smiling as he peers into her eyes that are as green as the sea and as hard to fathom.

As soft as a dove's cooing, she says, "Tell me the secret of your great strength. How can you be tied up and subdued?"

Her question surprises him. Is she toying with him? Playing a game? Or does she know something? Will she love him more if he tells her? Can she be trusted with his secret?

At her repeated requests, Samson finally gives in: "No razor has ever been used on my head, because I have been dedicated to God as a Nazirite, set apart to Him since birth. If my head were shaved, my strength would leave me."

Sensing she had heard the truth at last, Delilah waits until Samson falls asleep on her lap. Calling to Philistine conspirators hidden in the room, she signals a man to shave Samson's hair. When they are finished, she screams, "Samson, the Philistines are upon you!"

Jumping up to take them on just as he always had, Samson soon discovers he lacks the power to resist them. The Lord has left him. He is alone now and as weak as other men. Looking around for Delilah, he sees only the open door through which she has fled. Outside is darkness.[15]

• • •

He was the classic tragic hero—an otherwise strong human being destroyed by a single character flaw. Samson, the strongest man of his generation, a real "he-man," yet so pitifully vulnerable to pride, so tragically unable to conquer his tendency toward lust.

Yet God used this spiritually weak man. God used Samson's strength to keep the Philistines off balance and to keep the Israelite nation alive until she was ready for the next stage in God's redemptive purpose. God used the tragedy of Samson's life for good. God will have His way; He is the real superhero.

Can you relate to Samson? Is lust or pride threatening to bring you down? If so, then it's time to give your thought life a supernatural zap!

» TRIBAL TRAINING

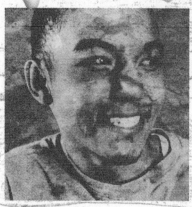

- **Get this: You're not alone in your struggles.** All guys of a certain age share the same desperate plea: "It's as if lust is controlling me! I beg God to forgive me, and I even promise to stop doing what I don't want to do. But then I fail—again and again. HELP!"

- **Understand the *real* problem.** The problem usually isn't what you think it is. Struggles with lust are almost always just mere symptoms. The *real problem* is actually a *heart problem*. And the only way to fix a mixed-up, sin-filled heart is by having a daily truth encounter. That means *spending time in the Word and in prayer*.

- **Saturate your mind with Scripture.** The Bible is more than just a bunch of letters printed on paper. (Remember "Living God's Word" on Day 5?) There is a supernatural component to the Bible that saturates our hearts and shapes our lives into what God wants them to be. Combine Bible reading with prayer and we've got a powerful weapon—an invisible sword, so to speak—that can fend off many deceptions and struggles that threaten to trap us.

- **Share your secrets with God.** Too many teens mistakenly believe that the Lord doesn't want them to be honest about their struggles. They think that He will be upset if they tell Him how they really feel. But if God already knows everything about you, even your secret sins can't make Him stop loving you. He wants you to experience His love, forgiveness, and power in all areas of your life if you'll only pour out your heart to Him.

- **PRAY IT OUT: "Lord, clean up my thought life and deliver me from lust and pride."** Ask Jesus to help you overcome your secret sins.

»TRIBAL MARKS

A Key Point I Learned Today:

How I Want to Grow:

Heart

Mind

Soul

Prayer List:

Family

Friends

Church

World Issues

Praise

Battles

Victories

Adventures

Day 12: Wait Training

»TRIBAL QUEST

Vow to remain sexually pure.

Explore the Word: Genesis 39:1–23, and 1 Corinthians 6:18–20

»TRIBAL TRUTH

Now Joseph was well-built and handsome, and after a while his master's wife took notice of Joseph and said, "Come to bed with me!" But he refused. . . . "My master has withheld nothing from me except you, because you are his wife. How then could I do such a wicked thing and sin against God?" And though she spoke to Joseph day after day, he refused to go to bed with her or even be with her.

—Genesis 39:6–10

»TRIBAL FACE

Joseph: Aspiring Governor of Egypt

Gone. The favored life Joseph had known since his childhood was gone forever. It happened in an isolated field far from his father's watchful eye. Betrayed by his brothers, sold into slavery, framed by his master's wife—was this some kind of test? Had the God of the universe abandoned him?

Joseph sits in a dungeon prison, waiting. The scenes replay over and over in his head.

Scene 1—The Betrayal: He is just a boy, trapped at the bottom of a dry well, stripped of the robe his father had given him. He can hear his older brothers plotting his murder. The fear, the sense of betrayal, the anguish of believing he will never see his father or his brother Benjamin again—his emotions feel raw and jagged inside.

His brothers rule out killing him and decide instead to sell him to traders bound for Egypt.[16]

Scene 2—Falsely Accused: Joseph ends up working as a slave at a palatial Egyptian oasis. His master, Potiphar, is a captain of Pharaoh's personal guard. Potiphar grows to trust Joseph but the captain's wife is another story.

One day, she whispers something. Words Joseph can hardly believe—a shocking invitation: "Hebrew boy, lie with me." Joseph ignores her.

Three days later, she tries again. She gazes at him from dead-level eyes, lids painted green with malachite. "Joseph," she entreats. "Lie with me."

Betray my master? Turn my back on God? Again, Joseph resists.

But Potiphar's wife persists. This time, she rushes at him and grabs his shoulder. Joseph runs, and his garment rips off in her hands. Joseph pauses—stunned and completely naked—then he darts into the courtyard.

She tells Potiphar Joseph has raped her and Potiphar has the teenager thrown into prison.[17]

Scene 3—God's Faithfulness: The blessings that landed him in Potiphar's household and put him in charge of everything Potiphar owned, continue even in prison, where the warden recognizes his abilities and puts him in charge of the other prisoners.

Joseph's memories are suddenly interrupted by keys clanging in the lock. Pharaoh has summoned him to court. He's heard that Joseph can interpret dreams.

"I have a dream," Pharaoh tells him, "and no one can interpret it . . ."

"I cannot interpret it myself," Joseph replies, "but God will give Pharaoh

the answer he desires." Joseph proceeds to explain that the dream predicts seven years of abundance followed by seven years of famine. He advises the ruler to store away a portion of food to prepare for the seven years of famine. Pharaoh is so pleased by Joseph's counsel that he declares, "Since God has made all this known to you, there is no one so discerning and wise as you. You shall be in charge of my palace, and all my people are to submit to your orders. Only with respect to the throne will I be greater than you." So Joseph becomes responsible for preparing Egypt for the coming famine.[18]

● ● ●

Joseph's life is more than a lesson in how to handle hard times; it's an example of solid "wait training." Because this young man waited on the Lord, never once compromising, God rewarded him.

When it comes to sexual purity, are you in a daily program of wait training?

As the editor of *Breakaway*, I read hundreds of letters each month on all kinds of topics. Many are from teens who don't want to wait for anything—guys whose lives are torn apart by regret and shame.

That's what happened to 16-year-old Daniel of Russellville, Arkansas. When I pulled his letter out of the envelope, I quickly discovered that it wasn't for me. He wrote it for you (and made me promise to print it).

Hey, Guys . . .

I'm writing to you about one of the most important decisions you will ever make—saving your body for your future wife.

Like me, you've probably heard a lot about abstinence, and you're probably getting tired of the topic. But listen carefully to what you hear. I sure wish I had.

About a year ago I failed God by not staying pure. At the time, I was reckless and really didn't care what happened to my life or anyone else's. I ended up having sex and tossing aside my virginity like an old rag. Even though God has forgiven me, it'll be a long time before I forgive myself (if ever).

When I saw the story about the abstinence cross a few months back, I felt like crying. I knew I had lost something precious—something I can never get back.

Listen, guys—I wish I'd never had sex. I'm more ashamed of this than anything I've ever done in my life. Stay pure.

—Daniel

The Problem: While God created sex as a beautiful gift to be shared only

in marriage, staying pure in this impure world is sometimes a struggle. (Perhaps the most difficult one a guy will ever face.)

The Answer: It comes from Scripture. Check out 1 Thessalonians 4:3–5: "It is God's will that you should be sanctified: that you should avoid sexual immorality; that each of you should learn to control his own body in a way that is holy and honorable, not in passionate lust like the heathen, who do not know God."

Need some help setting up a wait training program? Listen to Daniel, and take some clues from Joseph.

»TRIBAL TRAINING

- **Make a pact for purity.** Get your hands on a purity cross or ring as a sign of your choice to be pure.
- **Make it a team effort.** Take this stand with a buddy or two to hold each other accountable. Start by reading 2 Timothy 2:21–22, and then spend some time praying for each other.
- **Be totally honest about your struggles.** Take inventory of your life. Go down this checklist and take action where you need to:

Have you accepted God's forgiveness and stopped beating yourself up over past failures?

Have you talked to your dad (or if he's out of the picture, a relative, pastor, or youth leader) about your most intimate struggles?

Can you afford to change the way you think about the opposite sex?

Are you hanging on to any impure images (porn, raunchy mags, ads)?

- **Know the truth.** Keep in mind that sexual temptation is not sin. Some young men are weakened by guilt from temptation. A pure mind is not a mind free of temptation. A pure mind chooses to act in the right way when temptation strikes.
- **PRAY IT OUT: "Lord, help me to surrender my sexuality to You."** Ask Christ to sanctify your sexuality and give it back to you in all its glory and purity.

»TRIBAL MARKS

A Key Point I Learned Today:

How I Want to Grow:

Heart

Mind

Soul

Prayer List:

Family

Friends

Church

World Issues

Journal

Praise

Battles

Victories

Adventures

Day 13: Alien Nation

»TRIBAL QUEST

Vow to be an alien in this world, set apart by God to know and serve Him.
Explore the Word: 1 Peter 2:1–12

»TRIBAL TRUTH

Dear friends, I urge you, as aliens and strangers in the world, to abstain from sinful desires, which war against your soul. Live such good lives among the pagans that, though they accuse you of doing wrong, they may see your good deeds and glorify God on the day he visits us.

—*1 Peter 2:11–12*

»TRIBAL FACE

Samuel Morris: African Prince and Missionary

Samuel Morris feels like an alien in a strange world. In a very real sense,

he is. And the lean African teen knows that's how it has to be. That's how his Lord and Savior calls him to live.

It's the summer of 1891, and the 18-year-old is embarking on a daring journey to America aboard a tall sailing ship. It's much more than a voyage across the Atlantic. Samuel is moving from one world into another. He is on a quest to know and serve Jesus. Little does he realize, God is about to use him as a powerful voice against segregation and slavery.

Born in Liberia, West Africa, he was named Kaboo by his parents and is the eldest son of a tribal chieftain. Samuel is a prince in his country, but he ended up a prisoner. His life was held in torturous limbo until his father could repay his debts. While in captivity, he was forced to endure unbelievable cruelty. But just when death seemed imminent, he escaped and found new life through the compassion of Christian missionaries.

Today he, too, is a missionary—to the New World. Samuel leans over the railing of the ship and stares out at the horizon. All he can see in every direction is water and gentle waves. For nearly six months, the ocean has been his home. And it hasn't exactly been smooth sailing.

Here's how author W. Terry Whalin describes his voyage in her book, *Samuel Morris: The Apostle of Simple Faith:*

Only the day before, he had narrowly escaped death. Their ship, loaded with rich merchant cargo, was attacked. The men fought bravely and managed to beat off their attackers. But some of Samuel's friends on the ship were seriously wounded and others were killed.

His silent meditation on the water was broken with the beginning of a small church service at sea. The captain and his crew gathered on the deck. Samuel—or "Sammy," as his crewmates liked to call him—started the service by singing alone, "Jesus, our Shepherd, Brother, Friend, our Prophet, Priest, and King, our Lord, our Life, our Way, our End, accept the praise we bring."

After singing through this verse, Sammy stopped and asked the crewmen to join with him. During the singing, the bodies of the dead sailors were reverently lowered into the sea.

For weeks following the attack, Sammy was busy nursing the wounded and cleaning the ship. He didn't have time to wonder what would happen when he arrived in New York Harbor.

While in Africa, Sammy had learned about a man named Stephen Merritt. He'd decided to travel to America in order to meet Merritt and learn more about the Holy Ghost and a life that followed Jesus Christ. As the long voyage drew near the American coastline, the sailors began to question Sammy about his plans.

One of them asked, "How will you find your Stephen Merritt? Does he know you are coming?"

Another laughed, saying, "Do you think you can go into the city wearing those rags for clothes? We've got to do something about that!"

"I don't know. I don't know!" Sammy cried. "But my heavenly Father knows, and He will show me. Didn't He bring me to New York?" The crew nodded and had to admit defeat. They could see the determination in Sammy's eyes. There was no deterring this young man.

Suddenly the captain shouted, "Oh, Sammy come and see!" The captain pointed toward the distant shore. Sammy could see a statue of a woman holding a large torch. The captain explained, "The Statue of Liberty is a symbol of hope for the poor."

Sammy's face lit up with excitement—New York. The buildings of the city rose above the harbor like a bustling crowd.

"Well, we made it!" boomed the captain's voice. "And what a lovely Friday it is, too!" He smiled at Sammy. "You certainly earned your pay."

Tears fell from Sammy's eyes. It had been a Friday when he fled his captors. It had been a Friday when he had reached the settlement near Monrovia. And now he had arrived in New York on the same day.

"My emancipation day!" he cried joyfully. He turned his face toward heaven. "I thank You for this day, Father. I will ever dedicate Fridays to You. I will neither eat nor drink on this day, but will hunger and thirst after You."

• • •

Amazingly, Samuel found Stephen Merritt, a minister who operated a mission in New York City. In fact, on Samuel's first night in America, the teen ended up leading 17 homeless men to Christ! Merritt was overjoyed. This young man, who had virtually no formal education or training, was converting people whom the seasoned pastor had spent months trying to reach.

There was something amazing about Samuel—something alien and supernatural that brought people to their knees. Merritt knew exactly what it was: Christ in the boy. Samuel had been set apart by God. He had been empowered and sent to the United States to do the Lord's work.

»TRIBAL TRAINING

• **Live as an alien.** Crucial to knowing Jesus intimately and serving Him passionately, a Christian's walk, talk, and mindset simply cannot mirror the world. We're called to be different: "Do not conform any longer to the pattern of this world, but be transformed by the renewing of your mind" (Romans 12:2). Of course, this is much easier said than done. But there are some guys who aren't afraid to be different.

Nathanael, 17, from Farmington, Minnesota: "I'm a believer who will stand up and say that there should be a noticeable difference between Christians and non-Christians. The Bible gives an explanation of how a sincere Christian should act."

Josh, 16, from New Carlisle, Ohio: "Living as an authentic Christian means always being conscious of others' feelings, never putting others down, and not worrying so much about being cool or fitting in with the crowd. Above all, true Christians must have the guts to stand up for their beliefs."

• **Carry the cross.** In unmistakable language, Jesus told His followers that discipleship meant a life of self-denial and the bearing of a "cross." He asked them to count the cost carefully. Here's how author and evangelist Billy Graham explains it: "Jesus told His followers that the world would hate them. Even their loved ones would persecute them. He also warned, 'a time is coming when anyone who kills will think he is offering a service to God' (John 16:2). The Christian, therefore, must expect conflict, not an easy, cozy life. He is a soldier, as it has been said, and his captain never promised him immunity from the hazards of battle."[19]

• **PRAY IT OUT: "Lord, help me to be set apart as an alien in this world."** Ask Jesus for the courage to be different when it's safer to blend in. Ask Him to help you to take your eyes off the world. Ask Him for an eternal vision.

»TRIBAL MARKS

A Key Point I Learned Today:

How I Want to Grow:

Heart

Mind

Soul

Prayer List:

Family

Friends

Church

World Issues

Tribe: A Warrior's Heart

Journal

Praise

Battles

Victories

Adventures

RESISTING

Day 14: Resisting the Deceiver

»TRIBAL QUEST

When the Deceiver strikes and temptation heats up, turn to the Lord and His Word for the power to resist.

Explore the Word: Matthew 4:1–11

»TRIBAL TRUTH

Jesus said to him, "Away from me, Satan! For it is written: 'Worship the Lord your God, and serve him only.' " Then the devil left him, and angels came and attended him.

—Matthew 4:10–11

Tribe: A Warrior's Heart

»TRIBAL FACE

Jesus Overcomes the Devil

It's time. He is ready.

Filled with the Holy Spirit, Jesus journeys deep into the wilderness for some intense "tribal training." The Savior spends 40 days and nights trekking through the wastelands of Judea—alone, with no food or shelter. It's a savage, desolate terrain, a dangerous place. At night, the temperatures drop to bone-chilling digits. By midday the heat of the sun grows intolerable.

Weary and fighting the dull ache of starvation, Jesus begins the Test. Jesus is resting in a shady spot, the shadow of a boulder. His eyes are closed and He's leaning against the giant stone. Suddenly, He senses it—an icy presence, the presence of evil.

The Lord raises His head and squints. A few feet away, a flash of white light rises from the desert into the sky, the radiance of supernatural power. Slowly coming into focus within the center of this light is the image of a handsome man. The light is this curious figure.

With an arrogant, yet almost sympathetic tone, the light speaks. "Since You are God's Son, speak the word that will turn these stones into loaves of bread."[20]

At first, Jesus neither stands nor answers. He regards the light as though it were a savage beast sniffing too close to Him. Then He closes His eyes again, and in a hoarse voice whispers: "It is written, 'No one lives by bread alone, but by every word that issues from the mouth of God.'"

All at once, the cold presence completely engulfs Jesus. A wind arises and begins to howl. When the Lord opens His eyes, He finds that the light has completely surrounded Him, canceling the desert in a pale fog. Then He feels a footing beneath Him. He stands, and the light releases Him, moving to one side, and so Jesus is able to see that He has been transported to the highest corner of the temple wall. Scattered like pebbles below Him is the Holy City, Jerusalem. Here the priests blow trumpets to usher in the New Year. Here the air is thin and the height is giddy.[21]

The icy light speaks again. "Jump, and prove You are the Son of God." The presence goads Him, quoting Psalm 91: "For the Scriptures declare, 'God will send His angels to keep You from harm'—they will prevent You from smashing on the rocks below."[22]

Jesus counters with a citation from Deuteronomy: "It also says not to put the Lord your God to a foolish test!"

Resisting the Deceiver

In a flash, the Holy City vanishes, and Jesus is no longer on the temple wall. He is now infinitely higher than anything made by human hands. Standing on a cosmic mountain, the presence gestures expansively—pointing out all the earth's kingdoms, how glorious they all are. Then he says, "They're Yours—lock, stock, and barrel. Just fall down on Your knees and worship me, and they're Yours."[23]

But Jesus does not look at the kingdoms of the world, and His refusal is stern: "I know you. I know what sort of angel you are. Satan, tempter, betrayer—get out of here!" The Savior backs His rebuke with another quotation from Deuteronomy: "Worship the Lord your God, and only Him. Serve Him with absolute single-heartedness."

In an instant, Jesus is sitting in the desert again, leaning against a boulder. The test is over and the Devil is gone. In place of the icy presence are warmth and peace and goodness. Angels come down from heaven to care for the Savior.

• • •

Imagine the stress. If Jesus had slipped up just once, had committed even one little sin, it would have been over. There wouldn't have been a perfect Sacrifice to live and die in our place—and the world would not have been saved. Satan also knew this. So he used all of his strength and cunning to get Jesus to stumble.

Jesus had been in the wilderness nearly six weeks with no food. Naturally, He was struggling. And Satan was there with his first phase of attack: the temptation of immediate self-gratification.

"If You are the Son of God, tell these stones to become bread," he said. (In other words, "Let Your physical desires take control. If You're a man, why don't You have sex? If You're so cool, why do You turn down drugs?")

The trick failed, so Satan tried phase two: "All this I will give You, if You will bow down and worship me." ("Compromise, and You'll have it made. One lie, and Your parents will be off Your case. Cheat, and You'll pass.")

But failing again, Satan attacked Jesus once more—hard and heavy. But even though He was physically exhausted, Jesus won. How? He had powerful ammunition: the Word of God.

There's a definite supernatural power in the Scriptures. The Book of Ephesians lists the things we're to wear when we go into battle against the enemy. Most of the items are defensive. We're given the only offensive weapon we need, "the sword of the Spirit, which is the word of God"

(Ephesians 6:17).

Need help resisting the devil? Is temptation getting the best of you? Follow in our Savior's footsteps.

»TRIBAL TRAINING

• **Know the truth about Satan.** The Bible uses various names to describe Lucifer—Beelzebub, deceiver, lord of flies, serpent, dragon, fallen angel, enemy. Satan and his troops are viciously attacking the kingdom of God. His target: our souls. Yet as a created being, Satan is not a sovereign, all-powerful being, and he is certainly not equal to God. In the book *Essentials of Spiritual Warfare*, author A. Scott Moreau points out that Christianity is not a dualistic religion, a faith in which two opposing but equal powers struggle for control. "Even so, many Christians live as though Satan were as powerful as God," he writes. "Nothing could be further from the truth! . . . Because God is sovereign Satan does not stand a chance."[24]

• **Know the enemy's tactics.** Satan knows just which buttons to push to tempt you away from depending on Christ. He has watched your behavior over the years and knows where you are weak. That's where he attacks.

• **Know how to win the battle.** While you can't outsmart or outmuscle the flesh or the devil on your own, you can gain victory in your daily struggle against sin. The Lord has armed every Christian with spiritual weapons packed with "divine power": (1) the sword of the Spirit—the Holy Bible—and (2) prayer. Colossians 3:16 tells Christians to "let the word of Christ dwell in you richly," and Philippians 4:7 promises that "the peace of God . . . will guard your hearts and your minds in Christ Jesus."

• **PRAY IT OUT: "Lord, help me to resist the devil and to turn away from temptation."** Ask Jesus to protect you from Satan's evil schemes. Ask Him to give you victory over sin.

» TRIBAL MARKS

A Key Point I Learned Today:

How I Want to Grow:

Heart

Mind

Soul

Prayer List:

Family

Friends

Church

World Issues

Journal

Praise

Battles

Victories

Adventures

Becoming Like *Christ*

Day 15: Think Like Christ

»TRIBAL QUEST

H.D.J.T. (How Did Jesus Think)—that's what today's lesson is all about: establishing your identity and beliefs according to how Christ thought.

Explore the Word: Luke 2:41–52

»TRIBAL TRUTH

After three days they found him in the temple courts, sitting among the teachers, listening to them and asking them questions. Everyone who heard him was amazed at his understanding and his answers.

—Luke 2:46–47

»TRIBAL FACE

A Boy in the Temple

For guys in Jewish culture, a boy's twelfth birthday marks his passage into manhood and the beginning of some important new stuff to think about: establishing his identity, mission, and beliefs.

Jesus is 12, nearly 13, when His parents take Him to Jerusalem for the Feast of the Passover. Reaching Jerusalem from Nazareth requires a 4-day trek over harsh terrain where thieves and outlaws lurk, so many people from their town travel as a group.

When they arrive, Jerusalem is bursting with noisy celebration. Each day, hundreds of people stream in one temple gate with their sheep, while hundreds more stream out another—carrying bloody cuts of meat and the hide of the carcass of the animal they have sacrificed.

As the weeklong feast comes to a close, Mary and Joseph begin their grueling trip home. As Mary walks with the other women, she probably figures Jesus is with Joseph—while Joseph figures He's with her. It's quite a shock when they get together in the evening and discover He isn't with either of them.

Mary and Joseph first comb the camp and then spend three days searching the streets of Jerusalem. They hit all the festival attractions that should interest a boy of Jesus' age, never imagining that He'd be hanging out with religious scholars in the temple. But there He is, politely listening and asking questions of the top teachers—amazing all of them with His solid insights and answers.

Like any mom, Mary is upset when she finally lays eyes on her son. Here's how author Walter Wangerin, Jr., recreates the scene:

Mary flew around the pillars and found some 10 men sitting in a circle, old men, young men—and a boy! Rabbis, they were. Teachers and students and—

"Yeshi!" she shrieked. All talking came to a halt. "Yeshi, what are you doing here?"

Everyone turned and looked at her. Jesus turned, too, but with level eyes and a maddening calm.

A rabbi said, "The lad is studying the Law. He has a marvelous understanding—"

Mary hardly heard him. She ran to Jesus and took His face between her hands. "What have you done to us?" she hissed. She was going to cry. Therefore, she shouted at the top of her lungs: "Your father and I have been

Think Like Christ

searching the city for days! I would never have treated my parents like this! Yeshi, I've been dying with worry!"

"Mama," the boy said, "why did you have to search?"

"What? What are you saying?"

"But didn't you know where I would be? Didn't you know that I must be in my Father's house?"

Mary stopped shouting. She released her son's face, seeing pink marks where her hands had squeezed Him. No, she did not understand this thing which He said. Neither did she understand Him.[25]

• • •

"'Why were you searching for me?' he asked. 'Didn't you know I had to be in my Father's house?'" (Luke 2:49). These are the earliest words of Jesus quoted in the New Testament. Before this time, no one had ever referred to God as "My Father." No one had ever spoken about the Creator in such a personal, intimate way. From these few words, we discover a huge, myth-shattering truth about how our young Messiah thinks: *He knew His true identity was in serving God and doing His will.*

How does a 12-year-old already realize so much about His responsibilities? He knows He has a responsibility to His parents—but that His responsibility to do His Father's will comes first. He is not distracted by the fact that He knows His actions will cause His parents to worry. He accepts His place in life—He belongs in His Father's house. His focus is on eternity. Unlike other guys His age, selfish desires and living for the moment aren't even an issue.

Even though He was both fully human and fully God, Jesus was able to know completely who He was early in life. We can't understand it. No one knows how much He had to keep His frail, human side in check to stay committed to His values. But as a young man, Jesus shows He did understand who He was—a son to His parents. He returns home with Mary and Joseph, respecting their authority, and the fact that He's God's Son doesn't inflate His ego. He shows humility and still accepts His identity in both heaven and earth.

Even for Jesus, sometimes it was difficult to keep His responsibilities and beliefs straight. He understands our struggles because He went through them, too (remember His temptation in the wilderness?). Although He caused His parents worry, He never sinned. His journey to manhood was on the right path because His course was set by God.

So don't ever forget to ask yourself: *How Did Jesus Think?*

»TRIBAL TRAINING

• **Think differently about yourself.** In the world's eyes, your identity is wrapped up in who you know, what you do, how smart or athletic you are, or how you look. But in our heavenly Father's eyes, what matters is whose you are—His. God doesn't value anyone else in the world more than you. He knows you completely—better than you know yourself. And to Him, you are one-of-a-kind, priceless, and loved beyond belief. This truth alone should transform the way you see yourself.

• **Think about the truth.** Check out these can't-miss insights from J. I. Packer, a Christian scholar who has written a ton of life-changing books: "We were all created to be God's image-bearers. . . . We are made in such a way, I believe, that we are only at peace with ourselves when it's God's truth that our minds are grasping and consciously obeying. Human life is lacking dignity until you get to that point."[26]

• **Think about your values.** As a kid, you are told what to do by your parents. Maturity means standing up for what's right and living by your convictions—not what the crowd says is cool. When you have determined and prioritized your values, you will have confidence to move to the next step in the process of building the life you most desire. Consider where you have questions and commit to your search for truth: whether in the Bible, through a pastor, or in a trusted friend or family member.

• **PRAY IT OUT: "Lord, help me to think as Jesus thinks and to see myself as You see me."** Ask Jesus to give you courage to seek answers to your questions, the humility to accept them, and the faith to commit your desires fully to Him. Ask Him to bring the sources of His truth into your life that will mold you into the man He wants you to be.

Think Like Christ

»TRIBAL MARKS

A Key Point I Learned Today:

How I Want to Grow:

Heart

Mind

Soul

Prayer List:

Family

Friends

Church

World Issues

Praise

Battles

Victories

Adventures

Day 16: See Like Christ

»TRIBAL QUEST

Focus your vision to see others' needs with "eyes of compassion."

Explore the Word: Matthew 9:32–38

»TRIBAL TRUTH

As he approached the town gate, a dead person was being carried out—the only son of his mother, and she was a widow. And a large crowd from the town was with her. When the Lord saw her, his heart went out to her and he said, "Don't cry." Then he went up and touched the coffin, and those carrying it stood still. He said, "Young man, I say to you, get up!" The dead man sat up and began to talk, and Jesus gave him back to his mother.

—Luke 7:12–15

»TRIBAL FACE

Back from Death

Jesus pauses on the edge of Nain, a small town about a day's walk from Capernaum, and takes in a heartbreaking sight: a loud, but mournful, group heading to the local graveyard.

Professional mourners lead the procession clanging cymbals, playing flutes, and wailing. (It was sort of a custom in that day to hire these guys.) The mother walks alone behind this sad crowd. Men follow behind, carrying the coffin containing her dead son.

A mother losing her only child is a painful thought. What's more, the woman's husband is also dead. This means she's now completely alone. To whom will she turn? How will she survive? Who can possibly comfort her now? Her heartache and misery must be unbearable.

As Jesus' eyes meet hers, He is filled with compassion.

But, in this instance, Jesus does more than just feel sad. He stops the procession and exercises His authority over death, and something amazing happens. The boy comes back to life and crawls out of the coffin!

• • •

It's comforting to know that as we go through heartache, pain, and suffering, Jesus is right there by our side, feeling every tear, every ache, every bit of sorrow. And Jesus wants you to care about others in the same way. He wants you to see people with "new eyes."

While most Christian guys understand that their lives could—and *should*—be a reflection of Jesus Christ, they often allow fear of their peers to get in the way. But if God says we are worthy of His love, why do we pursue what our culture thinks is cool in order to feel good about ourselves?

The key is allowing the Holy Spirit and the truth of the Bible to saturate your heart, mind, and soul. Let the One who created you and everything else in this world reshape your heart, redefine your self-worth—and refocus your vision.

Are you ready for some "eye surgery"? It all begins by following Christ's example.

» TRIBAL TRAINING

• **Ask the Lord to show you how to be merciful, just as He is merciful.** Consider this: He reaches out to the unlovable, befriends those whom the world would rather forget, and touches those who seem untouchable. He sees their value.

• **Focus your vision.** Compassion is a core Christian quality, and next to Christ Himself, no other person on earth has come to represent the compassion of God more than Mother Teresa. As she has said, "We all long for heaven where God is, but we have it in our power to be in heaven with Him right now—to be happy with Him at this very moment. But being happy with Him now means loving like He loves, helping like He helps, giving as He gives, serving as He serves, rescuing as He rescues, being with Him 24 hours a day—touching Him in His distressing disguise."[27]

• **Step out of your "social safety zone."** Here's an opportunity to take a risk for God: Try showing some kindness to an outcast. (You know—the kid who sits alone in the back of the class; the one everybody else picks on.) Others may look down on you for associating with someone the crowd labels as "uncool." But the more you get to know the outcasts, the more you will begin to see with the eyes of compassion.

• **PRAY IT OUT: "Lord, teach me to see others the way You see them."** Ask Jesus to enable you to see a person's worth. Ask Him to help you commit to praying for your friends on a daily basis.

» TRIBAL MARKS

A Key Point I Learned Today:

How I Want to Grow:

Heart

Mind

Soul

Prayer List:

Family

Friends

Church

World Issues

See Like Christ

Praise

Battles

Journal

Victories

Adventures

Day 17: Love Like Christ

»TRIBAL QUEST

Learn what it means to "lay down your life" with authentic love.
Explore the Word: John 10:1–21

»TRIBAL TRUTH

"I am the good shepherd; I know my sheep and my sheep know me—just as the Father knows me and I know the Father—and I lay down my life for the sheep."

—*John 10:14–15*

»TRIBAL FACE

The Good Shepherd

There is no better picture of Jesus' deep love and total commitment to us than the illustration of a shepherd. The life of a dedicated shepherd means total devotion to his flock—a devotion that includes putting the sheeps' lives above his own.

First of all, there are thieves and robbers—dishonest men who try to lure stray lambs away from the flock and steal them. They aren't interested in the animals' welfare; they're only interested in the money they can get from them.

Sound familiar? Unfortunately there are more than a few of those folks around today—people who have turned Christianity into the business of bucks instead of the commitment of love.

But Jesus makes it clear that if we honestly seek God, we'll eventually be able to tell His voice from the crooks'.

Second, there are plenty of wild animals—mostly wolves. Whenever they close in, fierce and ravenous from hunger, the hired hands usually split. Why should they risk their lives for somebody else's property?

But the committed shepherd never looks upon his flock as "property." He's grown to know and love each of the sheep as individuals. In fact, his love and dedication to them is so intense that he would actually fight to the death to protect them.

Then there is the hazardous terrain on which the sheep graze—a dangerous landscape of holes, cliffs, and ravines. Knowing these pitfalls, the caring shepherd never pushes or drives his flock. Instead, he walks ahead of them, carefully scouting out the safest routes—gently leading them in areas he has already checked out.

Good pasture is also important. Grazing is about the only thing the sheep do, so why not make it as pleasant for them as possible? A sensitive shepherd goes to great risks to find the best grazing land for his sheep—to make their lives as happy and full as possible.

And finally, there are the hillside pens—places where the animals can gather for protection during the night. To make sure the sheep are really safe, the shepherd sleeps on the ground at the entrance of the pen. He will literally act as a human gate—a gate that serves as the only means to reach the flock.

• • •

By comparing Himself to a good shepherd, Jesus promises to care for us with a tender, intense, and all-giving love: He will protect us from evil, He will fight off any enemy that's trying to destroy us, He will go before us in every situation, and He will give us a happy and full life.

And guess what? As a Christian teen guy, the Lord wants you to share this same kind of radical love with the world. How?

It's Christ in you and the outpouring of His love through your words, your warmth, and your walk that will help others turn from evil. It's the Hero reflected in your face that will open their eyes to eternity. "God desires to take our

Love Like Christ

faces," writes Max Lucado, "this exposed and memorable part of our bodies, and use them to reflect His goodness."[28]

Are you sharing God's love with those around you? What do people see when they look at your life? Humility, kindness, goodness—a reflection of Christ's face? Follow Christ's example and show the world what true love is all about.

»TRIBAL TRAINING

- **Get a clue about how love is supposed to be expressed:** "Love is patient, love is kind. It does not envy, it does not boast, it is not proud. It is not rude, it is not self-seeking, it is not easily angered, it keeps no record of wrongs. Love does not delight in evil but rejoices with the truth. It always protects, always trusts, always hopes, always perseveres. Love never fails" (1 Corinthians 13:4–8).

- **Know this: God loves us even when we're unlovable.** He loves us unconditionally, without giving a second thought to our flaws and shortcomings. And that's how He wants us to treat others. When we love others unconditionally—forgiving them and reaching out to them—we are actually modeling His love.

- **Show kindness in your words and actions.** Do you communicate hope through the things you do or say? Do you know someone who gets sprayed with hateful graffiti—insults and put-downs?

Best-selling author Frank Peretti, a man who considers himself to be among the world's "walking wounded," warns Christians about verbal abuse: "It's like painting a sign around your neck: 'Beat up on me because you'll get away with it.' You begin to expect to be treated that way, and the other kids pick up on that like an animal smelling prey. That's how it was for me. My teen world was a virtual prison. Here's some advice for Christians of all ages: Have nothing to do with words that wound."[29]

- **PRAY IT OUT: "Lord, teach me how to share the love I experience through You with my friends—just as Christ 'laid down His life for His friends.'"** Ask Him to use your speech and actions as a clear message of God's salvation, grace, and love.

»TRIBAL MARKS

A Key Point I Learned Today:

How I Want to Grow:

Heart

Mind

Soul

Prayer List:

Family

Friends

Church

World Issues

Love Like Christ

Praise

Battles

Journal

Victories

Adventures

Day 18: Walk Like Christ

» TRIBAL QUEST

Strive to make serving, knowing, and following Jesus Christ your number-one passion.

Explore the Word: Luke 5:17–26

» TRIBAL TRUTH

"But that you may know that the Son of Man has authority on earth to forgive sins. . . ." He said to the paralyzed man, "I tell you, get up, take your mat and go home." Immediately, he stood up in front of them, took what he had been lying on and went home praising God. Everyone was amazed and gave praise to God. They were filled with awe and said, "We have seen remarkable things today."

—Luke 5:24–26

»TRIBAL FACE

A Paralytic Healed

"Who is this man?"

"The real question is, who does He think He is?"

The teachers of the Law had heard that Jesus was in town, stirring up the crowds with His radical ideas. A few of the skeptical religious leaders had to hear it for themselves—so they made their way into a crowded building and listened with disgust.

The young Jew before them claims to be the Messiah. He even insists that He has all authority on earth, yet He wanders the land like a drifter. What's more, He's a mere carpenter's son and hangs out with society's undesirables: lepers, beggars, prostitutes, traitors.

Suddenly . . . CREAK! SNAP! Wood breaks, clay falls, dust rises.

The Pharisees glare and look up.

A paralytic is lowered from the roof and gently placed at Christ's feet.

"Friend," Jesus says, "your sins are forgiven."

What did that man just say? wonders a teacher of the Law. He's blaspheming! Who can forgive sins but God alone?

Jesus looks at the Pharisee. "Why are you thinking these things?" He asks. "But that you may know that the Son of Man has authority on earth to forgive sins—"

Jesus turns to the crippled man. "I tell you, get up, take your mat and go home."

A miracle! The crowd gasps as the paralytic stands up and walks out the door. Everyone in the room rejoices. The teachers of the Law stare in shock.

• • •

Jesus became nothing so that we could have everything.

He wore a crown of thorns so that we might wear a crown of glory. He ate with men so we could someday dine with God. He became sin so that we might become righteousness. He cried tears on earth so we would never shed them in heaven. He walked over dusty roads so we could walk on golden streets.

He died so that we might live.

So who was this Man whose life—and death—changed the course of history?

No beauty. Isaiah foretold the agonies of Christ on the cross hundreds of years before Jesus was born. He also knew something about Jesus' appearance: "He had no beauty or majesty to attract us to him, nothing in his appearance that we should desire him" (Isaiah 53:2).

Walk Like Christ   115

If He had no outward beauty, then why were so many people attracted to Him? Christ's beauty was internal. His heart emanated unlimited love. The peace in His eyes drew crowds. The joy of His smile was contagious. Jesus didn't have good looks—He didn't need them.

No popularity. The Bible also describes Jesus as one who "made himself nothing, taking the very nature of a servant, being made in human likeness" (Philippians 2:7).

Christ was born in an animal shelter in the hick town of Bethlehem and was raised in the boondocks of Galilee by an average-joe carpenter. Later in life, in spite of the many times He helped others, people forgot to thank Him, asked Him to shove off, and tried to make Him look stupid. Those who hung around Him soon left, some of them running. If anything, Jesus had a bad reputation, bad enough to get Himself killed on a cross.

No sin. The Bible stamps the words "no sin" on the person of Christ three times:

1. "God made him who had no sin to be sin for us, so that in him we might become the righteousness of God" (2 Corinthians 5:21).

2. "He committed no sin, and no deceit was found in his mouth" (1 Peter 2:22).

3. "But you know that he appeared so that he might take away our sins. And in him is no sin" (1 John 3:5).

Christ had to be without sin to qualify as the perfect Sacrifice for the sin of mankind—the perfect Sacrifice for your sin. As God's sinless Sacrifice, Jesus made it possible for you to trust in Him and be forgiven.

Does He have your attention? Do you know Him?

»TRIBAL TRAINING

• **Don't be swayed by appearances.** As you know, things in this world are often not what they seem. But when you're seeing with eyes that look beyond appearances, you have a better chance of seeing what is good and bad for your spirit.

• **Hang out with Jesus.** My wife, Tiffany, and I have a solid relationship that's growing and deepening as each day passes. When we married, I knew I loved her deeply, next to my love for Jesus. And today, not only are we still in love, but we're also best friends. I'm proud of my wife and would lay down my life for her. I know she'd do the same for me.

Know what? My marriage also has taught me an important lesson about faith: Jesus wants us to have the same kind of deep, growing relationship with Him. When I spend time with my wife, our relationship grows. But if we neglect each other . . . you guessed it . . . our relationship suffers. (And if we continued on that dangerous course, our marriage would eventually die.) It's the same with your relationship with Jesus.

• **Strive to be holy "as Christ is holy."** *Holiness.* It's one of those words that conjures up images of uptight church ladies in floral dresses. It even brings to mind a long list of rigid, narrow-minded rules that are out of touch with reality—not to mention completely out of reach. Yet consider this: Scripture says, "Make every effort to live in peace with all men and to be holy; without holiness no one will see the Lord" (Hebrews 12:14).

But admit it: At times, your life seems to stray far away from anything that remotely resembles holiness. And the truth is, no one is born holy. So what's a weak, imperfect Christian to do? Turn to Christ for help. Take a look at what *The Message* says: "Here it is in a nutshell: Just as one person did it wrong and got us in all this trouble with sin and death, another person did it right and got us out of it. But more than just getting us out of trouble, he got us into life! One man said no to God and put many people in the wrong, one man said yes to God and put many in the right."[30]

• **PRAY IT OUT: "Lord, help me to know You better."** Ask Jesus to help you give up your own will for the will of God. Ask Him to enable you to daily live a life of spiritual sacrifice for the glory of Christ.

»TRIBAL MARKS

A Key Point I Learned Today:

How I Want to Grow:

Heart

Mind

Soul

Prayer List:

Family

Friends

Church

World Issues

Journal

Praise

Battles

Victories

Adventures

Day 19: Serve Like Christ

»TRIBAL QUEST

Accept Christ's call to care, always looking for ways to serve Him by serving others.

Explore the Word: John 13:1–17

»TRIBAL TRUTH

Jesus knew that the Father had put all things under his power, and that he had come from God and was returning to God; so he got up from the meal, took off his outer clothing, and wrapped a towel around his waist. After that, he poured water into a basin and began to wash his disciples' feet, drying them with the towel that was wrapped around him.

—John 13:3–5

»TRIBAL FACE

Foot Washer

Nearly one-third of the Gospel of John focuses on Christ's last few hours on earth—hours that, more clearly than any others in history, reveal the true personality of God.

Passover symbolism. Here it is, the Passover supper—the once-a-year meal celebrating how God freed the Jews from Egypt. But Jesus turns everything around and suddenly gives the meal a completely different meaning. In fact, in the other three Gospels (Matthew, Mark, and Luke), we see Him take portions of the supper, like the bread and wine, and explain how they no longer represent the people's freedom from Egypt. Instead, they are now to represent Him—His sacrificed body and shed blood that will free us from even tougher enslavement—enslavement to sin and its punishment.

The depth of God's love. Custom at this time calls for the host's servant to wash the guests' feet. But since there is no host where Jesus and His friends are eating, there is no servant. Other Gospel accounts talk about how the disciples have been arguing over which of them is the greatest—so there's a good chance most of them are pretty worried about who's going to end up with the bottom-of-the-barrel job of feet washing.

So, what does Jesus do? He strips down to what would be His underwear and begins washing each of the disciples' feet. Picture that for a moment— God, the Creator of the entire universe, kneeling and washing the smelly feet of men!

What a perfect picture. What a perfect example of God's heart—of the depth of His love and commitment to each of us.[31]

• • •

It is also a perfect demonstration of what God considers to be real greatness. It's not found in the world leaders, the professional athletes, the Hollywood superstars. It's not even found in the great spiritual leaders of our times. These aren't the ones whom God considers to be great. Instead, according to the Lord, "Whoever wants to become great among you must be your servant, and whoever wants to be first must be your slave—just as the Son of Man did not come to be served, but to serve" (Matthew 20:26–28).

Here's what author Henri J. M. Nouwen says about Christ's example of servanthood: "After washing His disciples' feet, Jesus says, 'I have given you an example so that you may copy what I have done to you' (John 13:15). After giving Himself as food and drink, He says, 'Do this in remembrance of Me' (Luke 22:19).

Jesus calls us to continue His mission of revealing the perfect love of God in this world. He calls us to total self-giving. He does not want us to keep anything for ourselves. Rather, He wants our love to be as full, as radical, and as complete as His own. He wants us to bend ourselves to the ground and touch the places in each other that most need washing. He also wants us to say to each other, 'Eat of me and drink of me.' By this complete mutual nurturing, He wants us to become one body and one spirit, united by the love of God."[32]

Are you ready for true greatness? Take some clues from Jesus and reach out to others . . . as a servant.

»TRIBAL TRAINING

• **Take the time to look around you.** Someone needs you. Someone at church, at school, at home. There's that 74-year-old man whose wife has Alzheimer's disease . . . he needs someone to talk to. Then there's that couple with a handicapped child . . . they really could use a break. You don't have to head off on a mission trip to Panama to serve God. Do it every day . . . in lots of little ways—such as taking the time to talk to that elderly man or volunteering to help that couple with their yard.

• **Be Christ's hands and feet.** From His birth to His death on a cross, Jesus' life is a shining example of humility and service. He reached out to those whom no one else wanted around. He brought love to the unloved, hope to the hopeless. How about you? Ask God to help you find at least one non-Christian person you can reach—through prayer, as well as service.

• **PRAY IT OUT: "Lord, break me and use me in ways that stretch way beyond my imagination."** Ask Jesus to help you get out of your comfort zone for a couple of weeks.

»TRIBAL MARKS

A Key Point I Learned Today:

How I Want to Grow:

Heart

Mind

Soul

Prayer List:

Family

Friends

Church

World Issues

Praise

Battles

Journal

Victories

Adventures

Day 20: Pray Like Christ

» TRIBAL QUEST

Make prayer a priority, believing in its power and trusting God for the outcome.
Explore the Word: John 17:1–26

» TRIBAL TRUTH

"I tell you the truth, my Father will give you whatever you ask in my name. Until now you have not asked for anything in my name. Ask and you will receive, and your joy will be complete."

—John 16:23–24

» TRIBAL FACE

Praying with Passion

The moment in which Jesus will fulfill His mission on earth is now less than 24 hours away, and He still has a lot to teach His disciples. The Lord especially wants His followers to get a clue about prayer.

"Ask the Father anything in My name, and I'll see to it that you get it—no ifs, ands, or buts. If you ask for anything in My name, it's yours."

But Jesus makes it clear that He's not a cosmic vending machine. We can't come to God with our shopping lists, slap on an "in Jesus' name I pray," then POOF! Our requests suddenly appear before our eyes.

"In Jesus' name" means just that. We are asking for things that are representational of who Christ is. We are asking for things that fit into His will and desires here on earth. And if our hearts—and motives—are right, then Jesus means exactly what He says: "I tell you the truth, my Father will give you whatever you ask in my name" (John 16:23).

A short time after saying all of this, Jesus looks toward heaven and begins

to pray (John 17:1–26). Probably no other section of Scripture more accurately captures the heart and deepest yearnings of Jesus than this prayer. He lets the disciples (and us) eavesdrop on His most intimate conversation with His Father.

Jesus prays for Himself. First, He asks to be glorified . . . "with the glory I had with you before the world began" (verse 5). Jesus is not on some power trip here. He knows that He is about to face more agony than any human being has ever faced in the history of the world—not just the pain of the cross, mind you, but the suffering and punishment for all the world's sins. For these few hours, He'll literally be carrying the weight of the entire world on His shoulders.

And He knows one other thing—He knows He can back out and call it quits any time He wants.

So He's praying for the strength and courage to go through with it, to succeed. If He does, there is no more perfect demonstration of God's love for us—or of His Son's immense glory.

Jesus prays for the disciples. Next, He begins praying for His friends. First, He asks for unity. It's as if He already knows the centuries of arguments and fights that are going to plague the church—everything from wars over major doctrines to hurt feelings about what color the curtains in the church bathroom should be.

Then He prays that even though the world may hate them, His followers will have the "full measure" of His joy (verse 13). Again Jesus makes it clear that real joy doesn't necessarily depend on outward circumstances. Real joy comes from the depth of our relationship with God.

Jesus prays for protection. Finally, He asks the Father to protect the disciples from the world. Not to take them out of the world—but to protect them while they're in it.[33]

• • •

Our Lord Jesus made prayer a priority in His life. And He often slipped away to be alone and to pray. In her book, Jesus, Man of Prayer, Margaret Magdalen writes: "Jesus needed the silence of eternity as a thirsting man in the desert needs water. . . . He longed for time apart to bask and sunbathe in His Father's love, to soak in it and repose in it. No matter how drained He felt, it seems that this deep, silent communion refreshed Him more than a good night's sleep."[34]

How about you? Does your faith need a soothing touch—or maybe a spiritual jolt? Follow Christ's example and make prayer a priority.

»TRIBAL TRAINING

•Don't make excuses—just pray!
Spend time alone with Jesus daily, and talk
to Him friend to friend. Pour out your heart
and tell the Lord about everything that's
going on in your life. Tell Him all your
dreams and desires—even your disap-
pointments. In the words of R. C. Sproul,
"The Lord God of the universe, the Creator
and Sustainer of all things, . . . not only
commands us to pray, but also invites us to
make our requests known. . . . In the act and dynamic of praying, I bring my
whole life under His gaze. Yes, He knows what is in my mind, but I still have
the privilege of articulating to Him what is there. He says, 'Come. Speak to
Me. Make your requests known to Me.' And so, we come in order to know Him
and to be known by Him."[35]

• Pray with the right motives. Popular author David Jeremiah explains it
this way: "God will not prostitute His power to give us desires that will in the
end be destructive to our walk with Him. But if we are consumed with a passion to find God's will through His Word and His Holy Spirit, we can always be
in the place where God can shower down His power upon us."[36] Also, praying
the Psalms is a great way to teach yourself how to pray in line with God's
nature and will.

• Follow Christ's example. He "went out to a mountainside to pray, and
spent the night praying to God" (Luke 6:12; see also Luke 5:16). He demon-
strated for us that intercession is central to a personal relationship with our
heavenly Father. He even told His disciples a parable "to show them that they
should always pray and not give up" (Luke 18:1).

• PRAY IT OUT: "Lord, teach me to pray." Ask Jesus to help you with
your commitment to pray. Ask Him to take away all your excuses, as well as
the distractions in your life, and begin connecting with Him through prayer.
Above all, dare to let Jesus talk to you daily in a way that could change your
life forever.

Tribe: A Warrior's Heart

»TRIBAL MARKS

A Key Point I Learned Today:

How I Want to Grow:

Heart

Mind

Soul

Prayer List:

Family

Friends

Church

World Issues

Pray Like Christ

Praise

Battles

Journal

Victories

Adventures

Day 21: Witness Like Christ

» TRIBAL QUEST

Learn to live an authentic faith, allowing your words and actions to be Christ's witness.

Explore the Word: Acts 1:6–11

» TRIBAL TRUTH

"All authority in heaven and on earth has been given to me. Therefore go and make disciples of all nations, baptizing them in the name of the Father and of the Son and of the Holy Spirit, and teaching them to obey everything I have commanded you. And surely I am with you always, to the very end of the age."

—*Matthew 28:18–20*

» TRIBAL FACE

Commissioning His Followers

Jesus' followers have just worshipped Him on the mountain near Galilee, and despite the fact that some disciples still have doubts in their hearts, Jesus commissions them and tells them to go out into the world.

"All authority in heaven and on earth has been given to Me," He tells them. "Therefore go and make disciples of all nations, baptizing them in the name of the Father and of the Son and of the Holy Spirit, and teaching them to obey everything I have commanded you."

Finally the time comes for Him to leave, to go and prepare a place for His followers and to send the Holy Spirit. He rises up into the clouds with the promise that He'll return in exactly the same way (see Acts 1:9–11).

• • •

Jesus was a Man on a mission. From sunup to sundown He healed the sick, cast demons out of people, and proclaimed that the day of liberation had come—absolute freedom from fear, from worry, from bad thoughts, from bad actions, from bitterness, from grief—from chasing after what the world claims is important.

The Divine walked among the destructive. And with Him came restored hope and healed hearts. Through His miracles, He told the world, "I am God, and I have brought you eternal life."

Jesus has commissioned us, too: "We are therefore Christ's ambassadors, as though God were making his appeal through us" (2 Corinthians 5:20).

The Lord didn't call us to hide in a Christian huddle—or to be part of His "secretive service." As Christians, we've grounded our lives on what the Bible says, which means we're convinced that humankind is more than just a cosmic accident. Jesus Christ is transforming our lives, and we've got to tell the world about it. Get this: *Those who don't know Christ are spiritually dead and are on their way to hell.*

But as you've probably already discovered, your assignment to be a witness isn't easy. The Enemy hates for believers in Christ to become burdened for the world. He knows that they'll begin to pray, give, and even go to the ends of the earth to share the good news about Jesus Christ. So he'll do anything he can to divert our attention.

But keep in mind that Christ is greater than the Enemy. Christ has put the Holy Spirit inside of each Christian; and every minute of every day, if we let Him, He'll continue to teach, guide, protect, and above all, love us and through us.

Are you willing to "get off your pew" and get going? If so, follow Christ's example and accept His call to "go" and "tell."

»TRIBAL TRAINING

• Don't be so uptight about witnessing. Too often, Christians fear they'll mess up in putting words to what God accomplished through the cross. We obsess over appearances and lose the purpose. We treat non-Christians like projects instead of people. We speak an alien language—known by insiders as "Christianese." The best thing we can do is relax and live what we believe, naturally, honestly, lovingly, and confidently. If we're comfortable with our faith, non-Christians will have a better chance of seeing Jesus in us.

• **Be bold.** We should never let fear hold us back from befriending an unbeliever. Seek to create relationships with nonbelievers. Consider the observations of legendary evangelist Billy Graham: "It is fear that makes us unwilling to listen to another's point of view, fear that our own ideas may be attacked. Jesus had no such fear, no such pettiness of viewpoint, no need to fence Himself off for His own protection. He knew the difference between graciousness and compromise and we would do well to learn from Him."[37]

• **Be ready with answers**—instead of just being polite and keeping quiet. Maybe your friend doesn't seem too interested in spiritual issues right now, but get this: He's watching you, especially your faith. And if he comes to you with a question one day, you need to speak up. "Always be prepared to give an answer to everyone who asks you to give the reason for the hope that you have" (1 Peter 3:15).

• **Have some "backbone."** Matthew 22:37–39 tells us to love others, but that doesn't mean tolerating their sin. (Of course, it doesn't mean wagging your finger at them either or being self-righteous.) Sometimes the best way of loving a nonbeliever is with the word NO—"No thanks, I don't smoke, drink, chew, (insert the appropriate word)"—then letting your backbone do the witnessing for you. "Do your best to present yourself to God as one approved, a workman who does not need to be ashamed and who correctly handles the word of truth" (2 Timothy 2:15).

• **PRAY IT OUT: "Lord, give me a heart and a passion for evangelism."** Ask Jesus to open your ears and eyes to the lost and to show you to whom you should reach out. Ask Him to give you the courage and the words that will open their eyes to His love and grace.

»TRIBAL MARKS

A Key Point I Learned Today:

How I Want to Grow:

Heart

Mind

Soul

Prayer List:

Family

Friends

Church

World Issues

Praise

Battles

Journal

Victories

Adventures

Fulfilling the Call

Day 22: Every Young Man's Heart

»TRIBAL QUEST

Commit your heart fully to Christ—relying upon His power, trusting His faithfulness, and knowing that "the battle is the Lord's."

Explore the Word: 1 Samuel 17:1–58

»TRIBAL TRUTH

David said to the Philistine, "You come against me with sword and spear and javelin, but I come against you in the name of the LORD Almighty, the God of the armies of Israel, whom you have defied. . . . All those gathered here will know that it is not by sword or spear that the LORD saves; for the battle is the LORD's, and he will give all of you into our hands."

—1 Samuel 17:45, 47

»TRIBAL FACE

David: Shepherd and Aspiring King of Israel

It's a jaw-dropping sight. Hillsides filled with thousands of jostling soldiers—voices shrieking, armaments clattering, spears flying.

Tribe: A Warrior's Heart

Suddenly, "RETREAT!" An entire battalion begins to scatter—all because of the presence of a single warrior.

Across the Valley of Elah stands a Philistine named Goliath, a giant of a man, nearly as tall as a basketball hoop is high. He's strong enough to wear 200 pounds of armor—including a bronze helmet and bronze leggings—and he's armed with a weapon that, in our time, might be mistaken for a torpedo: a bronze javelin several inches thick, tipped with a 25-pound iron spearhead.

Goliath shouts to the Israelites: "Do you need a whole army to settle this? I will represent the Philistines, and you choose someone to represent you, and we will settle this in a single combat! Send me a man who will fight with me!"[38]

For 40 consecutive days, Goliath's words rumble throughout the battlefield, striking fear in the hearts of the Israelite soldiers. Row after row of average, ordinary guys—with average height, average build, average faith—line the opposite hillside, gripping their spears with trembling hands, convinced that they've met their match. "There isn't a soul powerful enough to take on the taunting enemy across the valley."

The truth is, the Israelites are ordinary men who have forgotten one extraordinary thing: The Lord has chosen them as His warriors, the army of the living God.[39]

Another man steps up to the front lines—a much smaller, younger figure—a handsome teenager named David. He is the only Israelite who shows courage, the only one who sees the true battle being waged:

The arrogance of Goliath versus the power of God.

The faithlessness of Israel versus the faithfulness of God.

The dependence on human might versus the total reliance upon God.

"It is not by sword or spear that the Lord saves," David shouts to the giant, "for the battle is the Lord's."

A boy! Goliath is dumbfounded. New fury propels him forward, and he begins to charge downhill toward David. From across the battle line, the Philistine levels his spear at the lad's chest. But David doesn't flinch.

The teen's eyes are fixed on his target as he whirls a sling above his head, causing the leather to sing in the wind. With a snap, he releases it, and the stone rockets toward Goliath's skull. SMACK!

Suddenly, the champion of the Philistine armies slows to a walk, perplexed. He turns to the side, as if to ask a question, then topples backward upon the ground, like a great cedar felled.[40]

When the Philistines see that Goliath is defeated, they frantically pull their shields from the battle line and launch a hasty retreat. All Israel now raises a shout of triumphant joy.

• • •

It was a defining moment for David. This young man was convinced that no earthy giant, no mortal being, stood a chance against the all-powerful, immortal God of the universe. David got it right.

He chose to trust the God of Abraham, Isaac, and Jacob with unfettered courage. He seized life with great abandonment, confident that his Creator was directing his steps. And the boy who defended the Lord's people from a heartless thug grew into a "man after God's own heart" (see 1 Samuel 13:14).

Do you desire this kind of faith—this degree of rock-solid courage? Believe it or not, the Lord wired young men to have a heart like David's! Deep inside, we all yearn for something more. We crave a life of adventure and risk—to be a hero, to be a warrior, to know the Creator intimately.

So when the pressure hits, what seems to go wrong? Why do we retreat to fear instead of having faith?

»TRIBAL TRAINING

• **Don't let fear be a factor.** The next time you face an overwhelming obstacle, step into David's sandals: Hold tight to the promises of the Lord and stand firm with unwavering faith. As pastor Bill Hybels once remarked, "Don't spend a lot of time describing your mountain to the Lord. He knows what it is. Instead, focus your attention on the mountain mover—His glory, His power, and His faithfulness."

• **Let go—and let God!** Your heavenly Father wants you to learn how to handle hardships. In doing so, you'll begin to understand what it really means to step out as a "Christian." Commit right now to trusting Jesus with your whole heart. Ask Him to help you steer clear of the world's lies and be firmly grounded in His truth.

• **PRAY IT OUT: "Lord, help me to throw myself into Your arms with total abandonment."** Ask Jesus to give you a "warrior's heart." Ask Him to drive out doubt and fear and to mold you into a man of courage.

»TRIBAL MARKS

A Key Point I Learned Today:

How I Want to Grow:

Heart

Mind

Soul

Prayer List:

Family

Friends

Church

World Issues

Every Young Man's Heart

Praise

Battles

Tribe: A Warrior's Heart

Journal

Victories

Adventures

Day 23: Taking Eternal Risks

»TRIBAL QUEST

Step out of your comfort zone and be willing to risk all for the glory of God.

Explore the Word: 2 Corinthians 4:1–18

»TRIBAL TRUTH

But we have this treasure in jars of clay to show that this all-surpassing power is from God and not from us. We are hard pressed on every side, but not crushed; perplexed, but not in despair; persecuted, but not abandoned; struck down, but not destroyed.

—2 Corinthians 4:7–9

»TRIBAL FACE

Dr. David Livingstone: Explorer and Missionary

"Go!" This single command defines Dr. David Livingstone's life.

"Therefore go and make disciples of all nations, baptizing them in the name of the Father and of the Son and of the Holy Spirit" (Matthew 28:19).

Stay at home? Sit quietly in the safety of Scotland? Pursue a life of wealth and comfort? For this young doctor-turned-missionary, these aren't even options worth considering.

"Whatever way my life may be spent as best to promote the glory of our gracious God, I feel anxious to do it," he tells a friend as he sets off to Africa's vast Kalahari wilderness.[41]

It's the summer of 1841, and stretched out before him are endless savannahs, mysterious tribes, unsaved souls—and a God-sized assignment.

Dr. Livingstone never doubts his call to "take an eternal risk in Africa." The way he sees it, the gospel itself is the account of Jesus leaving His Father's right hand to go to Calvary. Likewise, Christ instructs those who want to be His disciples to leave their comforts and follow Him.

In a letter to his sister, Janet, Dr. Livingstone writes:

Tribe: A Warrior's Heart

Let us seek—and with the conviction that we cannot do without it—that all selfishness be extirpated, pride banished, unbelief driven from the mind, every idol dethroned, and everything hostile to holiness and opposed to the divine will be crucified; that "holiness to the Lord" may be engraven on the heart, and evermore characterize our whole conduct.[42]

In the years ahead, Dr. Livingstone's work proves to be painfully difficult, involving much personal sacrifice, lonely days away from his family—even countless life-threatening encounters in the African wilderness. His body soon bears the physical evidence of the suffering he must endure: His face, a leathery brown from exposure to the elements, is creased from the cares of a hard life, and his left arm is rendered useless—the result of a lion attack.

Yet after more than three decades of service, taking him 29,000 miles and providing him with many discoveries on his adventures, this Christian never strays from his mission to "prepare the way for the Lord."

"Shall I tell you what sustained me amidst the trials and hardships and loneliness of my exiled life?" Dr. Livingstone asks students at the University of Glasgow during a visit to Scotland. "It was a promise, the promise of a gentleman of the most sacred honor; it was this promise, 'Lo, I am with you always, even unto the end of the world.'"[43]

On May 1, 1873, Dr. Livingstone is found dead in his hut—his body kneeling by his bedside as if in the act of prayer, his head buried in his hands on a pillow. Next to him is a small, well-worn New Testament opened to Matthew 28. In the margin beside verse 20—the verse he shared with his students—is this notation: "The Word of a Gentleman."

• • •

God's promises sustained Dr. Livingstone. Often in the face of danger, Scripture would echo through his mind, breathing new hope into his soul—giving him the strength to endure the impossible. Dr. Livingstone understood that despite his weaknesses as a mere man, as a Christian, he had a treasure inside: Jesus Christ—the Source of spiritual muscle.

Today's Tribal Truth passage says it all. It's sort of mind-blowing to think about, isn't it? We're all like "jars of clay," often fragile and breakable. Yet the Lord actually reveals His limitless power and accomplishes His eternal work through our frail, mortal lives (like David's story about taking down a giant). But here's the deal: We must be willing—willing to follow, willing to be uncomfortable, and, above all, willing to risk everything.

So how about it? Will you leave your comfort zone and take a risk for eternity?

»TRIBAL TRAINING

• **Don't hide behind an excuse.** "But I don't know what to say. I'm not smart enough. I'm not strong enough." You've made the excuses. But God doesn't accept excuses. (Just ask Dr. Livingstone!)

• **Be willing to leave your comfort zone.** That invisible, safe circle we put around ourselves so we don't have to be bothered by anything or anyone? It's a selfish, protective cocoon that keeps us from being all God wants us to be. Besides, clinging to a safe, comfortable life can end up killing the soul.

• **Take eternal risks.** The thrill is there. The adrenaline flows. Your heart will race, but you'll also hear the God of the universe cheering you on—and that's the biggest thrill of all. So, what kinds of risks is God asking of you?

Speak the truth. Keeping quiet about creation (or purity or the pro-life cause) is easier, even safer. But speaking up is gutsy—and the right thing to do.

Tell your friends about Christ. It's definitely a risk, but a high and noble one. Sharing your faith means sharing your story: what you're all about, what Christ is all about, how He's helping you with your struggles.

Change your world. The possibilities are endless: You can get a group of friends together, then start a morning Bible study during the school year. You can collect old blankets from neighbors, then hand them out to homeless families in your town. You can start raising support now for a mission trip next summer. There will be more ideas for discerning God's purpose for you in Day 25.

• **PRAY IT OUT: "Lord, help me take risks for You—I am willing."** Ask Jesus to send you out of your comfort zone—out of what keeps you from following Him. Ask the Lord to reveal His face, His grace, and His hope through your life.

A Key Point I Learned Today:

How I Want to Grow:

Heart

Mind

Soul

Prayer List:

Family

Friends

Church

World Issues

Praise

Battles

Journal

Victories

Adventures

Day 24: The Freedom to Soar

»TRIBAL QUEST

Allow the Lord to "put wings on your desires," never letting failures, flops, and fumbles obscure His plans for you.

Explore the Word: Isaiah 40:21–31

»TRIBAL TRUTH

Do you not know? Have you not heard? The LORD is the everlasting God, the Creator of the ends of the earth. He will not grow tired or weary, and his understanding no one can fathom. He gives strength to the weary and increases the power of the weak. Even youths grow tired and weary, and young men stumble and fall; but those who hope in the LORD will renew their strength. They will soar on wings like eagles; they will run and not grow weary, they will walk and not be faint.

—Isaiah 40:28–31

»TRIBAL FACE

Captain Charlie Plum: Navy Pilot and P.O.W.

"It's time to 'rock 'n roll,'" Captain Charlie Plum says to a pilot-in-training.

The pressure hits as an F-18 Hornet Navy fighter jet descends to 500 feet above the earth, accelerates to 480 knots (530 MPH), and skims the ragged contour of the harsh desert below.

Today's mission: Charlie must coach a Navy trainee through some tricky low-level maneuvers.

The landscape becomes a reddish blur as Stash's 28-ton Hornet picks up speed. He navigates his craft through canyons and over hills—sometimes sideways, sometimes upside-down. Just when his trainee doesn't know which way is up or down, Charlie turns over the controls.

"No matter what conditions we face," he tells his trainee, "always trust the instruments. Understand?"

"Roger, sir," the young pilot responds.

The trainee examines the instruments, then squints out the window. The readings just don't feel right to him.

"Rocks ahead," shouts the captain. "Roll right. Unload." (Meaning: "You're gonna slam into a wall! Pull up and head out of the canyon.") After a couple of seconds of fumbling around, the trainee is still confused—and the plane continues on a collision course with a canyon wall. That's when Charlie takes over. The veteran pilot aggressively rolls the jet on its side and spirals out of the saddleback, barely missing a jagged ridge.

Once the plane has ascended to a safe height, the captain debriefs his student pilot. "You didn't listen to me," he stresses. "I'll say it again—NEVER go with your feelings in the air. Always trust the instruments."

"Yes, sir," the trainee says. "It's just that—"

"No excuses," Charlie barks. "The instruments will keep you on track. Now let's go in and do it again."

The trainee swallows hard. *This time, I'll do it right. This time, I'll trust the instruments.*

• • •

Unlike his fumbling, inexperienced students, Captain Charlie Plum—a legend among United States Navy pilots—could never be described as a failure. He put his life on the line in Vietnam during countless combat missions, he survived captivity (for six years) as a prisoner of war, and later in his career, Charlie helped to establish the Navy's elite Top Gun school in Southern California.

Yet it was a brush with failure during his teen years that helped mold him into the national hero he is today.

Growing up in Kansas, Charlie lived for basketball. He imagined one day leaving the wheat fields for fame and fortune in the NBA. But there was a tiny hitch in his big plan: He couldn't seem to lead his junior high team to a single win. After what felt like his "millionth loss," Charlie turned to his coach and poured out his heart: "I let you down—again. I guess I'm just a failure."

His stern mentor nodded in agreement and responded, "If that's what you believe, then I guess you are."

Puzzled, and a little shocked that his coach didn't offer encouragement during his dark moment, Charlie asked what he meant.

"Son, life is full of choices," the coach said. "If you choose to believe that you're a failure, and get stuck in this sort of mindset, then that's probably how you'll turn out. But if you choose to handle adversity with the right attitude—

The Freedom to Soar

if you strive to grow from failure—then you'll ultimately be a winner."[44]

That advice changed Charlie's life. Though this young man never found stardom in professional sports, he grew up to be a military hero. And the coach's words were put to the ultimate test behind enemy lines.

So which path will you choose? Are you willing to trust God—and allow Him to turn a stinging flop into a soaring success? Are you able to forget your imperfect past and look to the future with hope?

» TRIBAL TRAINING

• **Be willing to fail as you strive for success.** Often the moments in life that truly mold our character are those filled with embarrassing flops and fumbles, not shining triumphs. And the key to survival—and ultimately success—is faith. Christian scholar A. W. Tozer explains it this way: "God may allow His servant to succeed when He has disciplined him to a point where he does not need to succeed to be happy. The man who is elated by success and cast down by failure is still a carnal man. At best his fruit will have a worm in it."[45] Read that again.

• **When you blow it, don't make a second mistake: turning your back on God.** He's always there—reach out to Him. The Lord wants to transform tremendously flawed young men into winners who are fit to accomplish His purpose. Don't let life's blunders get in the way. Instead, let God have His way.

• **Learn from guys who have been there.** Turn to the Book of Judges for snapshot after snapshot of raw, uncensored *failure*—and God's gracious, divine deliverance. "Then the Israelites did evil in the eyes of the LORD and served the Baals" (Judges 2:11). Keep reading through chapter two and you'll discover that, despite humankind's gross unfaithfulness, God is faithful. He molds and disciplines His children. He shows persistent, unwearied love and matchless grace—grace that's absolutely underserved. "Then the LORD raised up judges, who saved them out of the hands of these raiders" (Judges 2:16).

• **PRAY IT OUT: "Lord, help me to soar—even when I fail."** Ask Jesus to give you a positive mindset and a heart that's faithful to Him, regardless of your circumstances. Ask Him to pick you up when you fall.

»TRIBAL MARKS

A Key Point I Learned Today:

How I Want to Grow:

Heart

Mind

Soul

Prayer List:

Family

Friends

Church

World Issues

Praise

Battles

Tribe: A Warrior's Heart

Journal

Victories

Adventures

Day 25: A Life with Purpose

»TRIBAL QUEST

Allow God to shape your character, building your faith, preparing your heart—and ultimately revealing His purpose for your life.

Explore the Word: Genesis 12:1–9

»TRIBAL TRUTH

"I will make you into a great nation and I will bless you; I will make your name great, and you will be a blessing."

—Genesis 12:2

»TRIBAL FACE

Abraham: Shepherd and "Father of a Nation"

Abram enters his tent, drops the door flap and kneels before a clay fire-pot. He blows on a coal until it glows, then touches it to the wick of a saucer lamp. A soft flame sparks, illuminating his weary face—lean and streaked with the dust of recent travel.

The old man stares at the flame, lost in thought. Then it happens. God speaks. Abram kneels silently—and listens.

"Leave your country," the Lord tells him, "leave your people and your father's household, and go to the land I will show you."

A short time later, Abram awakens his wife.

"Sarai, Sarai," he whispers, his face ashen, his eyes smoky and enormous, his voice ghostly. "Prepare to leave."

"Leave? Where? Is your father sick again?"

"The Lord God has commanded me to go," the old man insists. "He has made marvelous promises. Come now, we've got to leave—"[46]

Abram embraces the unknown and obeys. With nothing to guide him but a voice that whispers, "Follow Me," he and his family pull up their roots, flee all that is safe and familiar to them, and set off on an amazing journey. They travel through a hostile land, where there is famine and death. But Abram is patient and holds firm to his faith.

"I will make you into a great nation and I will bless you," the Lord promises Abram. "I will make your name great, and you will be a blessing."

God prospers Abram—and fulfills His promise.

• • •

An assignment from heaven whispered into the heart of a human—and the divine journey begins. That's the way a life with God starts. A voice says, "Follow Me." If the man is obedient to God's will, he gets up and follows.

God said He would make Abram's name great so that He could make him a blessing to future generations. Then, over the next 25 years, God developed Abraham's character to match the name He had given him.[47] Each time the Lord spoke, Abraham did his best to obey. Time and time again, he stepped into the unknown, clinging to the hope in his Creator.

The Lord has spoken to you, too. Are you listening? How will you answer?

»TRIBAL TRAINING

• **Discern God's will.** When you have a close relationship with Jesus—which is nurtured through prayer and Bible study— He will tell you Himself what He wants you to do. Not only does the Lord lead you to solid answers in Scripture, He also communicates with you throughout the day, answering your questions and guiding your steps. You literally walk in His presence minute by minute. The Holy Spirit deals with each human being in a personal and intimate way, convicting, directing, and influencing us. How? Think about those times when you faced a temptation of some sort. (Maybe it was lying or stealing . . . or lust.) Remember how that "something inside" seemed to kick in, telling you to turn away? More than likely, "that something" was the Holy Spirit directing you obey to the will of God. Of course, the Lord gave you a free will to follow Him—or to disobey.

Bottom line: As you grow closer and closer to Him, your instincts will become more sensitive to His influence. Your entire mind and spirit will become more in tune to God, and you'll begin to hear Him more clearly, just as you would with any good friend.

• As you pray and seek God's will, be prepared to wait. God has promised to speak to our hearts, so we can expect Him to, but He is not compelled to tell us everything we want to know the moment we desire the information. It can take time for God to speak. By causing us to wait, He prepares us for His answer, which we may have missed had He spoken immediately. We have to be prepared to listen. Remember Dr. Tozer's comment from Day 24 about how God shapes and prepares us? (Go back and read it again if you need to.) Be patient as God molds your character. These times may draw out and stretch your faith, but as popular author Henry T. Blackaby points out, "He will take whatever time is necessary to grow your character to match His assignment for you. . . . Character-building can be long and painful. It took 25 years before God entrusted Abraham with his first son and set in motion the establishment of the nation of Israel. Yet God was true to His Word."[48]

• When the Lord whispers "GO!"—be faithful to obey. If you follow God, you will find what Abraham discovered: What he left behind was nothing compared to what lay ahead. You will walk on a path filled with the solid promises of God. Your life will take on greater meaning and purpose—a whole new purpose for living. A whole new power to live in the joy of sins forgiven and wounds healed. A whole new degree of strength for the moment and hope for tomorrow.

PRAY IT OUT: "Lord, shape my character as You prepare me to fulfill Your purpose." Ask Jesus to grow you into a young man who is far stronger, far more obedient than you presently are. Ask Him to show you how to be faithful with the small assignments—always preparing you to handle even bigger tasks.

»TRIBAL MARKS

A Key Point I Learned Today:

How I Want to Grow:

Heart

Mind

Soul

Prayer List:

Family

Friends

Church

World Issues

A Life with Purpose

Praise

Battles

Tribe: A Warrior's Heart

Journal

Victories

Adventures

Day 26: The Author of Dreams

»TRIBAL QUEST

Commit your dreams and desires to God—allowing Him to write your story. *Explore the Word: Proverbs 16:1–22*

»TRIBAL TRUTH

All a man's ways seem innocent to him, but motives are weighed by the LORD. Commit to the LORD whatever you do, and your plans will succeed. The LORD works out everything for his own ends. . . . When a man's ways are pleasing to the LORD, he makes even his enemies live at peace with him. Better a little with righteousness than much gain with injustice. In his heart a man plans his course, but the LORD determines his steps.

—*Proverbs 16:2–4, 7–9*

Tribe: A Warrior's Heart

C.S. Lewis: Scholar and Writer

"Here on the mountain I have spoken to you clearly: I will not often do so down in Narnia. Here on the mountain, the air is clear and your mind is clear; as you drop down into Narnia, the air will thicken. Take great care that it does not confuse your mind. And the signs which you have learned here will not look at all as you expect them to look, when you meet them there. That is why it is so important to know them by heart and pay no attention to appearances. Remember the signs and believe the signs. Nothing else matters."[49]

Aslan, the great talking lion in "The Chronicles of Narnia," speaks these powerful words to a young adventurer about to set off on a quest. The life-changing wisdom leaps from the pages to reveal timeless truths in our own world as well.

This, of course, is precisely the intent of the books' author, C.S. Lewis.

The signs, ponders Lewis as he sips from a teacup and scribbles the dialogue for his next Narnian tale, *The Silver Chair,* in his Oxford, England, study.

Remember the signs and believe the signs. Nothing else matters.

Aslan's words, in a very real sense, are the essence of Lewis' soul. The story he is telling carries a deeper, eternal message—one we all long to hear; one we're actually all helping to create with our lives. The signs he describes point to the ultimate truth: the gospel of Jesus Christ. Aslan is a symbol as well, and much more than just the king of Narnia—he is symbolic of the King of kings.

"Supposing," Lewis asks himself, reflecting on the nature of God, the sufferings of Christ, and other fundamental Christian truths, "that by casting all these things into an imaginary world, stripping them of their stained-glass and Sunday school associations, one could make them for the first time appear in their real potency. . . ."[50]

And so Lewis sets out to do just that in "The Chronicles of Narnia." And many years in the future (October 1963 to be exact), long after the Narnia stories have been published, he writes to a young reader who catches the deeper meaning of Aslan's words. *If you continue to love Jesus, nothing much can go wrong with you, and I hope you may always do so. I'm so thankful that you realized the "hidden story" in the Narnian books. It is odd, children nearly always do, grownups hardly ever.*[51]

In reality, C.S. Lewis is one of those grownups who, for much of his early

The Author of Dreams

life, didn't get the "hidden story" either. At age 17, Jack—better known to the world as C.S. Lewis—explained bluntly to Arthur Greeves, a Christian friend he'd known since childhood, "I believe in no religion. There is absolutely no proof for any of them, and from a philosophical standpoint Christianity is not even the best."[52]

Then, in September, 1931, the truth began to sink in—that is, with the help of his best friend, author J.R.R. Tolkien. It starts on the grounds of Magdalen College, Oxford, England. Here's how author Jim Ware recreates the scene in his book, *God of the Fairy Tale*:

Two tweed-jacketed, pipe-puffing professors go crunching down the gravel path known as Addison's Walk, under the deeper shadows of a grove of trees.

"Look!" says one of them, a tall, long-faced fellow with the furrowed brow and twinkling eyes of a sage . . . or wizard. He points to a large oak. "There it stands," he says, "its feet in the earth, its head among the stars. A majestic miracle of creation! And what do we call it? A tree." He laughs. "The word falls absurdly short of expressing the thing itself."

"Of course it does," responds the other, a round-faced, slightly balding, bespectacled man in his mid-30s. "Like any word, it's just a verbal invention—a symbol of our own poor devising."

"Exactly," says the first man. "And here's my point: Just as a word is an invention about an object or an idea, so a story can be an invention about Truth."

The other rubs his chin. "I've loved stories since I was a boy," he muses. . . .

"But don't you see, Jack?" persists his friend. "The Christian story is the greatest story of them all. Because it's the real story. The historical event that fulfills the tales and shows us what they mean. The tree itself—not just a verbal invention."

Jack stops and turns. "Are you trying to tell me that in the story of Christ . . . all the other stories have somehow come true?"[53]

• • •

Fifteen years after his declaration to Arthur Greeves, and a week and a half after his conversation with Tolkien, Lewis finally believed "the signs" and was transformed by the truth. He wrote to that same friend—Arthur Greeves—with a very different outlook: "I have just passed on from believing in God to definitely believing in Christ—in Christianity. My long night talk with Tolkien had a great deal to do with it."

God gave you eyes so that you might see, ears so that you might hear, a will so that you might choose, and a heart so that you might live. "I have come that they may have life," Jesus said, "and have it to the full" (John 10:10). But if you are to become who you were born to be, if you truly desire to let God write your story, you must find what the Creator has set in your heart—just as C.S. Lewis eventually did.[54]

Consider this challenge from popular author John Eldredge: "Instead of asking what you ought to do to become a better man . . . ask what makes you come alive? What stirs your heart?"[55]

»TRIBAL TRAINING

- **Let God be the Author of your dreams.** Do some serious soul-searching and think about your dreams, desires, and all the things that genuinely stir your heart. List them on a piece of paper, then commit them to prayer.

- **Take to heart Aslan's advice:** During life's daily stresses—especially when questions of "right and wrong" get fuzzy—do you "remember the signs"? Do you seek the truth of God as you make decisions?

- **Make plans for your life, but realize that the Lord may have a different path for you.** Remember the apostle Paul? Before God changed him, he wanted to spend his life wiping out Christianity. However, from Paul's birth, God had planned for him to be His greatest missionary: "For you have heard of my previous way of life in Judaism, how intensely I persecuted the church of God and tried to destroy it. . . . God, who set me apart from birth and called me by his grace, was pleased to reveal his Son in me so that I might preach him among the Gentiles" (Galatians 1:13, 15–16).

- **PRAY IT OUT: "Lord, determine my steps."** Ask Jesus to reveal what His good, pleasing, and perfect will looks like for you. Ask Him to help you fit yourself into what God wants for you rather than what you want for yourself.

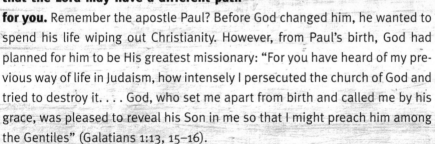

»TRIBAL MARKS

A Key Point I Learned Today:

How I Want to Grow:

Heart

Mind

Soul

Prayer List:

Family

Friends

Church

World Issues

Journal

Praise

Battles

Victories

Adventures

The Author of Dreams

Day 27: Heroic Faith

»TRIBAL QUEST

Be willing to "lay down your life" for the cause of Christ, allowing Him to mold you into a courageous Christian.

Explore the Word: Philippians 1:12–29

»TRIBAL TRUTH

I eagerly expect and hope that I will in no way be ashamed, but will have sufficient courage so that now as always Christ will be exalted in my body, whether by life or by death. For to me, to live is Christ and to die is gain.

—Philippians 1:20–21

»TRIBAL FACE

Jim Elliot: Missionary and Martyr

He is no fool who gives what he cannot keep to gain what he cannot lose.

Jim Elliot writes these words during his youth, never imagining that he'll one day immortalize them—with his very life.

Many years later, Jim and four friends—Peter Fleming, Ed McCully, Nate Saint, and Roger Youderian—are in the middle of a lush green jungle in Ecuador. It's a deceptive place: beautiful on the surface, yet dangerous at its core. It's a land filled with deadly animals and hostile tribes—a forgotten corner of the world that these men are determined to reach with the gospel.

Jim and his ministry team set up camp on the edge of the Curaray River—then wait. The young missionary's heart is racing as he anticipates the moment, the fulfillment of years of prayer and planning. He is about to make contact with a primitive people group known as the Auca Indians.

"They aren't even called by their right name among the tribes we have already reached," Jim had told the other missionaries before their excursion. "The Quichua call them 'Auca,' which means 'simply savages' in the Quichua tongue. Everyone seems to echo that they are deathly afraid of outsiders and will shoot first and ask questions later. They will kill anyone for simply setting foot in their part of the forest."[56]

Jim and his colleagues know the risks they're facing. But each man is committed to the mission: Step out with courage and share the eternal hope

of Jesus Christ.

Nate radios his wife: "Pray for us! We're sure we'll have contact today! Will radio you again at 4:30."

Many miles away, the missionary wives gather around their radio later that afternoon. But 4:30 comes and goes with no word from the ministry team. Something has gone wrong. The next day, a search party makes its way to the river camp. What they find shocks the world.

In her book, *Shadow of the Almighty*, Jim's wife, Elisabeth Elliot, sums up what happened:

Committing themselves and all their carefully laid plans to Him who had so unmistakably brought them thus far, they waited for the Aucas. Before 4:30 that afternoon, the quiet waters of the Curaray flowed over the bodies of the five comrades, slain by the men they had come to win for Christ, whose banner they had borne. The world called it a nightmare of tragedy. The world did not recognize the truth of the second clause in Jim Elliot's credo: "He is no fool who gives what he cannot keep to gain what he cannot lose."[57]

• • •

News of the martyred Christians made headlines in major newspapers throughout the world. Reporters bombarded the missionary families with endless questions: How did these men die? What went wrong? Weren't these five Christians foolish to attempt befriending such a savage Indian tribe? Wasn't this nothing more than a tragic waste of lives?

When the relationship between the Huaorani tribe and the missionaries was more solidified some time later, these questions were posed to one of the men who had been involved in the killing of the five martyrs. He explained that up until that time, all of their contact with outsiders had involved killing or trying to kill one side or the other, and for this reason their fear of outsiders often prompted them to attack before the others attacked them. In the case of these five white men, the villagers had greatly wondered why they wanted to make contact with them—what profit did they hope to extract from their tribe? They instinctively feared a trap.[58]

Not long after the attack, the Huaorani began to understand their mistake. They remembered the actions of one of the missionaries: "He had a revolver, and used it to fire some warning shots," a tribesman explained. "The men had weapons, yet refused to use them to harm us. Why?"

When the villagers had finally heard the story of Jesus—how He had given His life to reconcile man to God—they immediately understood the

actions of the five missionaries. The Huaorani had believed the gospel preached, because they had seen the gospel lived.[59]

God wants you to live what you believe—to embrace the world with heroic faith. While He may never ask you to go to the extremes of guys like Jim Elliot, He does want you to "lay down your life in love" (see John 15:12–13).

Are you willing?

»TRIBAL TRAINING

• **Freely give "what you cannot keep."** Our love for others is evidence of our love for God. And the Lord wants us to give it away daily. Here's what the late Christian artist Rich Mullins had to say about Christian love: "What marks us as Christians is our love for people. And if you love people you respect them. No one was ever won into the kingdom through snobbery. We come to know Christ through love. I think you can profess the Apostles' Creed until Jesus returns, but if you don't love somebody you never were a Christian."[60]

• **Know that heroic faith has "backbone."** Remember, loving others doesn't mean tolerating sin or wagging our fingers at people. Sometimes you'll have to say NO—and let your backbone do the witnessing for you.

• **Strive to "gain what you cannot lose."** How? By getting your eyes off the moment, and seeing with an eternal perspective. So, the next time you're in a tight spot, ask yourself this question: Am I willing to throw away what's right and settle for stuff that's wrong, just to please the crowd? "Do your best to present yourself to God as one approved, a workman who does not need to be ashamed and who correctly handles the word of truth" (2 Timothy 2:15).

• **PRAY IT OUT: "Lord, give me heroic faith."** Ask Jesus to help you live selflessly—always willing to "lay down your life in love." Ask Him to give you the courage to live what you believe.

»TRIBAL MARKS

A Key Point I Learned Today:

How I Want to Grow:

Heart

Mind

Soul

Prayer List:

Family

Friends

Church

World Issues

Heroic Faith

Praise

Battles

Tribe: A Warrior's Heart

Journal

Victories

Adventures

Day 28: Committed to the Call

»TRIBAL QUEST

Strive to "burn your ships," staying committed to God—His ways, His Word, and His will.

Explore the Word: John 14:15–31

»TRIBAL TRUTH

"Whoever has my commands and obeys them, he is the one who loves me. He who loves me will be loved by my Father, and I too will love him and show myself to him."

—John 14:21

Tribe: A Warrior's Heart

Hernando Cortes: Captain and Explorer

It's a grueling journey, and the fleet of 11 ships is battered almost beyond repair. Even harder hit are the nerves of the crew.

"Has our captain gone mad?!" yells a sailor.

"He'll end up getting us all killed," complains another.

"I say we turn around and GO BACK!" insists a crewman.

Suddenly, fear erupts on the decks. "GO BACK! GO BACK! GO BACK! Let's go back to the life we once knew."

But Hernando Cortes won't budge. He has amassed his battalion of 508 soldiers and 100 sailors and has set out on an important quest for the king of Spain: Explore the New World.

Cortes silences the crowd. "Gentlemen, we can't go back now. This is our destiny. We were made for this moment."

Then he reminds his men of the words he had printed on a banner: "Brothers and comrades, let us follow the sign of the Holy Cross in true faith, for under this sign we shall conquer."

It works. And soon the ships reach Mexico.

Yet Cortes doesn't let out a sigh of relief. He knows other storms are just on the horizon. So he quickly goes to work, disciplining his army, shaping it into a cohesive force.

Then the famous conquistador does something that will be retold again and again in the history books: He orders his men to burn the ships.

By doing so, Cortes actually saves the lives of his crew. Since the ships are so weather-beaten from the journey, returning to Spain would be risky—even suicidal. And by that single action, Cortes commits himself and his entire force to survival through conquest. It also ensures that they keep their eyes on the New World, not on the life they left behind.

• • •

As Christians, Jesus has called us to burn our ships, too.

Following Him involves a lifetime commitment. We have come to a whole new world through our relationship with Christ—and there's no turning back. But nobody said it would be easy (not even Christ).

Do you sometimes have doubts about the Lord's power in your life? If so, maybe it's time to commit and "burn the ships."

It's God's plan that we move toward the goal of becoming more like His Son, Jesus Christ. This is a big goal; that's why God gave us a lifetime to work on it. But it all begins by burning the ships and keeping your eyes on the New World, not on the life you left behind.

»TRIBAL TRAINING

- **Follow the compass.** Jesus knows there will be hardships and times when we wish we could go back to "safer" ground. Remember that He is there for you. He'll help you through the tough times. He won't sit idly by, hoping you'll have the strength to withstand. He wants to provide the inner muscle it takes to combat the outer pressure you feel. You can call out God's name and talk to Him directly! The fact is that the Almighty God, Creator of the universe, King of kings, Knower of all things, loves you more than you'll ever imagine. (He's your biggest fan.)

- **Stay on course.** The shallow Christian simply hides his Bible, purchases a wardrobe of "couch potato" T-shirts, and then lives up to what's written on his chest. His favorite book is A Lazy Man's Path to Heaven. And since this guy knows God is forgiving, he thinks his ticket is paid. But Jesus wants you to be a person of depth. He doesn't want you to sell out for what's comfortable or go back to the old life you once knew.

- **Drop anchor in Christ.** Open your eyes to the incredible future that awaits you. The Lord is calling you to plug in to His power through prayer and Bible study, and set your sights on a greater world ahead. "The people of the world focus on what they are overcoming," writes Henry T. Blackaby. "Christians focus on what they are becoming."[61]

- **PRAY IT OUT: "Lord, help me to be committed to the call."** Ask Jesus to conform you into His image. Ask Him to help you "burn your ships"— doubt, fear, bitterness, unbelief—and let go of the past. Tell God that you want to focus on your future with Him.

»TRIBAL MARKS

A Key Point I Learned Today:

How I Want to Grow:

Heart

Mind

Soul

Prayer List:

Family

Friends

Church

World Issues

Committed to the Call

Praise

Battles

Journal

Victories

Adventures

Survivor Stuff #1

»Tribal Treasure Map
(How the Bible Is Organized)

Here's a tribal trek through the Scriptures!

The Holy Bible is like an ancient map that leads to treasure. But to find the treasure, you've got to know how to read the map. In reality, this big, black, leather-bound "life map" is a library of 66 books, or booklets, bound into a single volume and divided into two primary collections of books:

The Old Testament

This is the first collection—39 books—which teaches us the basics about life and creation, about God's commitment to us, the prophecies of the Messiah, and why we need Christ: Sin is a failure to attain the standard God has set, a perversion of our nature, a breaking of God's holy law, and rebellion against our Creator.

The Old Testament is divided into:

The Pentateuch (Genesis to Deuteronomy)—the foundation of the Bible—tells us who God is, what He does for us, and what He requires of us; it instructs us in God's laws.

The history books (Joshua to Esther)—chronicle man's rebellion and God's faithfulness.

The poetry books (Job to the Song of Solomon)—demonstrate the wonder, the mystery, and the majesty of God.

The major prophets (Isaiah to Daniel)—declare the holiness of God; they provide a foreshadowing of the Good News to be brought by Jesus.
The minor prophets (Hosea to Malachi)—point to devastation, idolatry, cruelty, and the ultimate coming of the Messiah.

The New Testament

This is the second collection of books in the Bible—27 books written by ten different authors. The New Testament begins with the four Gospels, and includes a record of the spread of the Good News preached by Jesus, as well as letters to individuals and churches, and general letters that read like sermons. The last book, Revelation (or the Apocalypse), tells of the final triumph of Jesus and the judgment of all humanity.

»Tribal-Truth-in-a-Year Reading Plan

Follow the daily readings listed here, and you'll have the whole Bible read in one year! You will definitely be changed by what God teaches you through His Word.

Week 1 • Genesis 1–3 • Genesis 4–5 • Genesis 6–8 • Genesis 9–11 • Genesis 12–14 • Genesis 15–17 • Genesis 18–20

Week 2 • Matthew 1–4 • Matthew 5 • Matthew 6 • Matthew 7 • Matthew 8–10 • Matthew 11–13 • Matthew 14–15

Week 3 • Genesis 21–23 • Genesis 24–27 • Genesis 28–30 • Genesis 31–36 • Genesis 37–41 • Genesis 42–45 • Genesis 46–50

Week 4 • Matthew 16–18 • Matthew 19–20 • Matthew 21–23 • Matthew 24–25 • Matthew 26–28 • Mark 1–3 • Mark 4–6

Week 5 • Exodus 1–4 • Exodus 5–7 • Exodus 8–12 • Exodus 13–18 • Exodus 19–24 • Exodus 25–31 • Exodus 32–34

Week 6 • Mark 7–8 • Mark 9–10 • Mark 11–12 • Mark 13 • Mark 14–16 • Luke 1–3 • Luke 4–6

Week 7 • Exodus 35–40 • Leviticus 1–7 • Leviticus 8–10 • Leviticus 11–17 • Leviticus 18–22 • Leviticus 23–25 • Leviticus 26–27

Week 8 • Luke 7–8 • Luke 9–10 • Luke 11 • Luke 12 • Luke 13–14 • Luke 15–16 • Luke 17–18

Week 9 • Numbers 1–4 • Numbers 5–9 • Numbers 10–14 • Numbers 15–21 • Numbers 22–25 • Numbers 26–31 • Numbers 32–34

Week 10 • Luke 19–21 • Luke 22 • Luke 23 • Luke 24 • John 1–2 • John 3–4 • John 5–6

Week 11 • Numbers 35–36 • Deuteronomy 1–5 • Deuteronomy 6–11 • Deuteronomy 12–16 • Deuteronomy 17–20 • Deuteronomy 21–26 • Deuteronomy 27–30

Week 12 • John 7–8 • John 9–10 • John 11–12 • John 13–14 • John 15–17 • John 18–19 • John 20–21

Week 13 • Deuteronomy 31–34 • Joshua 1–4 • Joshua 5–8 • Joshua 9–12 • Joshua 13–19 • Joshua 20–24 • Judges 1–3

Week 14 • Judges 4–8 • Judges 9–12 • Judges 13–16 • Judges 17–21 • Ruth 1–4 • 1 Samuel 1–3 • 1 Samuel 4–7

Week 15 • Acts 1–4 • Acts 5–7 • Acts 8–11 • Acts 12–15 • Acts 16–18 • Acts 19–21 • Acts 22–28

Week 16 • 1 Samuel 8–12 • 1 Samuel 13–15 • 1 Samuel 16–17 • 1 Samuel 18–20 • 1 Samuel 21–26 • 1 Samuel 27–31 • 2 Samuel 1–4

Week 17 • Romans 1–3 • Romans 4–5 • Romans 6–8 • Romans 9–11 • Romans 12–16 • 1 Corinthians 1–4 • 1 Corinthians 5–6

Week 18 • 2 Samuel 5–7 • 2 Samuel 8–10 • 2 Samuel 11–12 • 2 Samuel 13–14 • 2 Samuel 15–20 • 2 Samuel 21–24 • 1 Kings 1–4

Week 19 • 1 Kings 5–8 • 1 Kings 9–11 • 1 Kings 12–16 • 1 Kings 17–19 • 1 Kings 20–22 • 2 Kings 1–7 • 2 Kings 8–10

Week 20 • 1 Corinthians 7 • 1 Corinthians 8–10 • 1 Corinthians 11–14 • 1 Corinthians 15–16 • 2 Corinthians 1–3 • 2 Corinthians 4–7 • 2 Corinthians 8–9

Week 21 • 2 Kings 11–13 • 2 Kings 14–17 • 2 Kings 18–21 • 2 Kings 22–25 • 1 Chronicles 1–9 • 1 Chronicles 10–12 • 1 Chronicles 13–17

Week 22 • 2 Corinthians 10–13 • Galatians 1–2 • Galatians 3–4 • Galatians 5–6 • Ephesians 1–3 • Ephesians 4–6 • Philippians 1

Week 23 • 1 Chronicles 18–21 • 1 Chronicles 22–27 • 1 Chronicles 28–29 • 2 Chronicles 1–4 • 2 Chronicles 5–9 • 2 Chronicles 10–13 • 2 Chronicles 14–16

Week 24 • Philippians 2 • Philippians 3 • Philippians 4 • Colossians 1–2 • Colossians 3–4 • 1 Thessalonians 1–3 • 1 Thessalonians 4–5

Week 25 • 2 Chronicles 17–20 • 2 Chronicles 21–24 • 2 Chronicles 25–28 • 2 Chronicles 29–32 • 2 Chronicles 33–35 • 2 Chronicles 36 • Ezra 1–2

Week 26 • 2 Thessalonians 1–2 • 2 Thessalonians 3 • 1 Timothy 1 • 1 Timothy 2–3 • 1 Timothy 4–6 • 2 Timothy 1–2 • 2 Timothy 3–4

Week 27 • Ezra 3–6 • Ezra 7–8 • Ezra 9–10 • Nehemiah 1 • Nehemiah 2–3 • Nehemiah 4–7 • Nehemiah 8–10

Week 28 • Titus 1 • Titus 2 • Titus 3 • Philemon • Hebrews 1–2 • Hebrews 3–4 • Hebrews 5–7

Week 29 • Nehemiah 11–13 • Esther 1–3 • Esther 4–6 • Esther 7–10 • Job 1–7 • Job 8–14 • Job 15–19

Week 30 • Hebrews 8–10 • Hebrews 11–13 • James 1 • James 2 • James 3–5 • 1 Peter 1–2 • 1 Peter 3–4

Week 31 • Job 20–24 • Job 25–31 • Job 32–37 • Job 38–42 • Psalm 1–4 • Psalm 5–8 • Psalm 9–12

Week 32 • 1 Peter 5 • 2 Peter 1 • 2 Peter 2 • 2 Peter 3 • 1 John 1–2 • 1 John 3–4 • 1 John 5

Week 33 • Psalms 13–16 • Psalms 17–20 • Psalms 21–24 • Psalms 25–28 • Psalms 29–32 • Psalms 33–36 • Psalms 37–41

Week 34 • 2 John–3 John • Jude • Revelation 1–3 • Revelation 4–5 • Revelation 6–7 • Revelation 8–11 • Revelation 12–14

Week 35 • Psalms 42–45 • Psalms 46–49 • Psalms 50–53 • Psalms 54–56 • Psalms 57–59 • Psalms 60–62 • Psalms 63–65

Week 36 • Revelation 15–16 • Revelation 17–20 • Revelation 21–22 • Ecclesiastes 1–2 • Ecclesiastes 3–5 • Ecclesiastes 6–8 • Ecclesiastes 9–12

Week 37 • Psalms 66–68 • Psalms 69–72 • Psalms 73–75 • Psalms 76–78 • Psalms 79–81 • Psalms 82–84 • Psalms 85–89

Week 38 • Song of Songs • Isaiah 1–6 • Isaiah 7–12 • Isaiah 13–18 • Isaiah 19–23 • Isaiah 24–27 • Isaiah 28–31

Week 39 • Psalms 90–92 • Psalms 93–95 • Psalms 96–98 • Psalms 99–101 • Psalms 102–104 • Psalms 105–106 • Psalms 107–109

Week 40 • Isaiah 32–35 • Isaiah 36–39 • Isaiah 40–48 • Isaiah 49–52 • Isaiah 53–55 • Isaiah 56–59 • Isaiah 60–66

Week 41 • Psalms 110–112 • Psalms 113–115 • Psalms 116–118 • Psalm 119 • Psalms 120–124 • Psalms 125–129 • Psalms 130–134

Week 42 • Jeremiah 1–6 • Jeremiah 7–10 • Jeremiah 11–15 • Jeremiah 16–20 • Jeremiah 21–24 • Jeremiah 25–29 • Jeremiah 30–33

Week 43 • Psalms 135–137 • Psalms 138–140 • Psalms 141–144 • Psalms 145–150 • Proverbs 1 • Proverbs 2 • Proverbs 3

Week 44 • Jeremiah 34–38 • Jeremiah 39–45 • Jeremiah 46–52 • Lamentations • Ezekiel 1–3 • Ezekiel 4–11 • Ezekiel 12–17

Week 45 • Proverbs 4 • Proverbs 5 • Proverbs 6 • Proverbs 7 • Proverbs 8 • Proverbs 9 • Proverbs 10

Week 46 • Ezekiel 18–24 • Ezekiel 25–32 • Ezekiel 33–39 • Ezekiel 40–48 • Daniel 1–3 • Daniel 4–6 • Daniel 7–12

Week 47 • Proverbs 11 • Proverbs 12 • Proverbs 13 • Proverbs 14 • Proverbs 15 • Proverbs 16 • Proverbs 17

Week 48 • Hosea 1–3 • Hosea 4–5 • Hosea 6–10 • Hosea 11–14 • Joel 1–2 • Joel 3 • Amos 1–2

Week 49 • Proverbs 18 • Proverbs 19 • Proverbs 20 • Proverbs 21 • Proverbs 22 • Proverbs 23 • Proverbs 24

Week 50 • Amos 3–6 • Amos 7–9 • Obadiah • Jonah • Micah 1–2 • Micah 3–5 • Micah 6–7

Week 51 • Proverbs 25 • Proverbs 26 • Proverbs 27 • Proverbs 28 • Proverbs 29 • Proverbs 30 • Proverbs 31

Week 52 • Nahum • Habakkuk • Zephaniah • Haggai • Zechariah 1–8 • Zechariah 9–14 • Malachi

Survivor Stuff #2

Notes

[1]Greg Hartman, "The Heavens Declare His Glory," *Breakaway* magazine, July 1999, 29–30.

[2]Bill Myers and Michael Ross, *Faith Encounter* (Eugene, Ore.: Harvest House, 1999), 112–113.

[3]J. I. Packer, *J. I. Packer Answers Questions for Today* (Wheaton, Ill.: Tyndale House, 2001), 11.

[4]Matt Redman, *The Unquenchable Worshipper* (Ventura, Calif.: Regal, 2001), 113.

[5]dcTALK, *Jesus Freaks II* (Minneapolis: Bethany, 2002), 226–227.

[6]Ibid., 229–230.

[7]Henry T. Blackaby, *Experiencing God Day-by-Day* (Nashville: Broadman & Holman, 1998), 257.

[8]Dietrich Bonhoeffer, *The Cost of Discipleship* (New York: Collier, 1959), 47–49.

[9]Walter Wangerin, Jr., *The Book of God* (Grand Rapids: Zondervan, 1996), 845.

[10]Ann Spangler and Robert Wolgemuth, *Men of the Bible* (Grand Rapids: Zondervan, 2002), 371.

[11]Kenneth J. Collins, *A Real Christian: The Life of John Wesley* (Nashville: Abingdon, 1999), 51.

[12]John Wesley, Journal, 24 May 1738, in *A Diary of Readings*, ed. John Baillie (New York: Collier, 1955), 73.

[13]Gerald G. May, M.D., *Addiction and Grace* (San Francisco: Harper Collins, 1988), 3–4.

[14]Adapted from Ted Huston, *More Than Mountains: The Ted Huston Story* (Portland, Ore.: Pacific, 1995).

[15]Adapted from Spangler and Wolgemuth.

[16]Ibid.

[17]Wangerin, 83.

[18]Adapted from Spangler and Wolgemuth.

[19]Billy Graham, *The Faithful Christian: An Anthology of Billy Graham* (New York: McCracken, 1994), 33–34.

[20]Eugene H. Peterson, *The Message Remix: The Bible in Contemporary Language* (Colorado Springs: NavPress, 2003), 1770.

[21]Wangerin, 623.

[22]Ted Miller, *The Story* (Wheaton, IL: Tyndale, 1986), 316.

[23]Peterson, 1770.

[24]A. Scott Moreau, *Essentials of Spiritual Warfare* (Wheaton, IL: Harold Shaw, 1997), 51.

[25]Wangerin, 613.

[26]Packer, 11.

[27]Mother Teresa, *Contemplative in the Heart of the World* (Ann Arbor, MI: Servant, 1985), 114.

[28]Max Lucado, *Just Like Jesus* (Nashville: Word, 1998), 200.

[29]Tom Neven, "Teenage Torture," *Breakaway* magazine, October 2002, 6.

[30]Peterson, Romans 5:18–19.

[31]Myers and Ross, 197–198.

[32]Henri J.M. Nouwen, *Show Me the Way* (New York: Crossroad, 1995), 130–131.

[33]Myers and Ross, 197–198.

[34]Margaret Magdalen, *Jesus, Man of Prayer* (Downer's Grove, IL: InterVarsity, 1987).

[35]R. C. Sproul, *Effective Prayer* (Wheaton, IL: Tyndale, 1984).

[36]David Jeremiah, *Sanctuary* (Nashville: Integrity, 2002), 53.

[37]Billy Graham, *Unto the Hills* (Dallas: Word, 1986), 123–124.

[38]Miller, 142.

[39]Dirk R. Buursma and Verlyn D. Verbrugge, *Daylight Devotional Bible* (Grand Rapids: Zondervan, 1988), 293.

[40]Wangerin, 259.

[41]J. H. Worcester, Jr., *The Life of David Livingstone* (Chicago: Moody, n.d.), 14.

[42]Sam Wellman, *David Livingstone—Missionary and Explorer* (Uhrichsville, OH: Barbour, n.d.), 41.

43Harold Sala, *Profiles in Faith* (Uhrichsville, Ohio: Barbour, 2003), 12–13.

44Michael Ross, *Faith That Breathes* (Uhrichsville, Ohio: Barbour, 2003), 256–257.

45A. W. Tozer, *Tozer on Christian Leadership: A 366-Day Devotional* (Camp Hill, Penn.: Christian Publications, Inc., n.d.), reading for October 19.

46Wangerin, 18.

47Blackaby, 16.

48Ibid.

49C.S. Lewis, *The Silver Chair* (New York: Harper Collins, 1953), 27.

50From "Sometimes Fairy Stories May Say Best What's to Be Said," in *Of Other Worlds,* ed. Walter Hooper (New York: Harcourt Brace Jovanovich, 1966).

51C.S. Lewis, "Letter to Ruth Broady," dated October 26, 1963, in *Letters to Children,* ed. Lyle Dorsett (New York: Macmillan, 1985), 111.

52C.S. Lewis, *They Stand Together: The Letters of C.S. Lewis to Arthur Greeves* (New York: Macmillan, 1979), 135.

53Jim Ware, *God of the Fairy Tale* (Colorado Springs: WaterBrook, 2003), 1–3.

54Note: Much more has been written on C.S. Lewis's writing and his conversion to Christianity. Check out: *The Most Reluctant Convert* by David C. Downing; *C.S. Lewis: Lightbearer in the Shadowlands* by Angus J.L. Menuge; and *C.S. Lewis* by Ruth James Cording.

55John Eldredge, *Dare to Desire* (Nashville: J. Countryman, 2002), 34.

56Dave and Neta Jackson, *Hero Tales: A Family Treasury of True Stories from the Lives of Christian Heroes, Volume 2* (Minneapolis: Bethany, 1997), 45.

57Elisabeth Elliot, *Shadow of the Almighty* (New York: Harper & Row, 1958), 18–19.

58dcTALK, 273.

59Ibid., 274.

60Christopher Coppernoll, *Soul2Soul* (Nashville: W Publishers, 1998), 47, 49.

61Blackaby, 315.

⌃ The author with his son at Yosemite National Park.

AUTHOR BIO

Michael Ross is the editor of *Breakaway,* a national magazine for teen guys published by Focus on the Family. Communicating with teenagers and families is his passion. He is a speaker and a columnist for *Living With Teenagers* magazine (LifeWay). Michael is also the author of more than 16 books for young people, including *BOOM: A Guy's Guide to Growing Up* (Tyndale) and *Faith that Breathes* (Barbour).

Michael also loves adventure travel. His most memorable trip was a safari through Zimbabwe by motorcycle (with a bunch of teens, of course), then by boat down the Zambezi River. Each summer, he and the staff of Summit Adventure (a California-based wilderness ministry) take teen guys on 10-day backpacking excursions near Yosemite National Park.

Michael and his wife Tiffany live in Colorado Springs with their young son, Christopher, and two cats.

Check out www.breakawaymag.com. You'll find lots of great stuff from *Breakaway* magazine, including advice from Michael's monthly "HEY MIKE!" column and info on how you can join the "tribe" on *Breakaway's* wilderness adventures.

Tools for the tribe!

At Focus on the Family, we are committed to helping you learn more about Jesus Christ and preparing you to change your world for Him! We realize the struggles you face are different from your parents', or your little brother's, so we've developed a bunch of stuff especially for you!

We don't want to tell you what to do. We want to encourage and equip you to be all God has called you to be in every aspect of life. That may involve strengthening your relationship with God, solidifying your values, and perhaps making some serious changes in your heart and mind.

We'd like to come alongside as you consider God's role in your life, discover His plan for you in the lives of others, and learn to impact your generation to change the world.

We have Web sites, magazines, palm-sized topical booklets, fiction books, a live call-in radio show—all dealing with the topics and issues that you deal with and care about. For a more detailed listing of what we have available, visit our Web site at www.family.org. Then click on "resources," followed by "teen guys."

» LIFE ON THE EDGE LIVE!
A RADIO TALK SHOW FOR YOU

This award-winning national radio call-in show gives teen guys something positive to tune in to every Saturday night at 9 p.m. ET. You'll get a chance to talk about the hottest issues— no topic's off limits. Log on to www.lifeontheedgelive.com to find a station near you.

» PLUGGED IN

This montly magazine offers parents and youth leaders reviews and commentary on the latest music, movies, TV and other forms of entertainment aimed at youth.

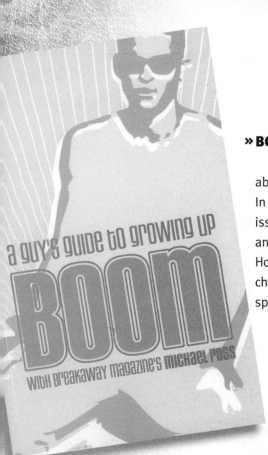

» BOOM: A GUY'S GUIDE TO GROWING UP

Where do you go when you have questions about life and the changes you're going through? In *BOOM: A Guy's Guide to Growing Up,* all the issues facing today's guys are addressed and answered in this easy-to-read, engaging book. Honest and straightforward, *BOOM* tackles physical changes, sexuality and dating, money management, spiritual growth, and more. Paperback.

» JUST FOR GUYS

In *Breakaway* magazine, you'll have somewhere to turn when the stress of peer pressure and growing pains crashes in on you. Packed with awesome graphics, engaging columns, and inspiring articles, it's a definite cool read! You'll get the lowdown on sports, celebrities, and girls—not to mention advice, humor, and spiritual guidance.

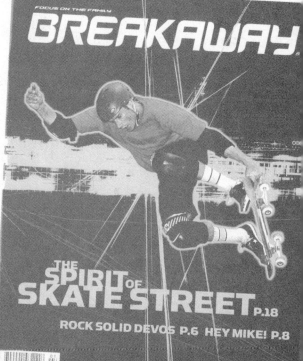

» BREAKAWAY'S SUMMIT ADVENTURES

FEAR IS NOT A FACTOR!

Throughout the Bible, God took His followers into the wild, away from their normal routines and out of their comfort zones to teach and shape them into godly men. This summer, join other guys for 10 days of backpacking, rock climbing and outdoor survival that will change your life.

THE TRIBE: We're recruiting guys age 14 and older who are ready to take their faith to a higher level. While wilderness experience isn't necessary, you MUST be in good physical condition.

PURE ADVENTURE: Under the guidance of Summit Adventure, a veteran Christian outdoor ministry, you'll trek through California's Ansel Adams Wilderness Area (near Yosemite National Park), climb and rappel down steep rockfaces, build friendships with other guys your age and nurture leadership abilities through intense faith-building lessons.

DON'T GET LEFT BEHIND: Download an application and info packet from www.breakawaymag.com— or send for one by writing us at this address: ***Breakaway's* Summit Adventure, 8605 Explorer Drive, Colorado Springs, CO 80920.**